SCHOPENHAUER'S
TELESCOPE

Gerard Donovan

COUNTERPOINT

COUNTERPOINT IS A MEMBER OF THE PERSEUS BOOKS GROUP
NEW YORK

Copyright © Gerard Donovan, 2003

First published in Great Britain by Scribner, 2003, An imprint of Simon &
Schuster UK Ltd A Viacom Company

First hardcover edition published in the United States in 2003 by
Counterpoint Books, a member of the Perseus Books Group, 387 Park
Avenue South, New York, NY 10016-8810. Counterpoint's edition is
published by arrangement with Simon & Schuster.
First U. S. paperback edition published in 2004 by Counterpoint.

The right of Gerard Donovan to be identified as author of this work has
been asserted by him in accordance with sections 77 and 78 of the
Copyright, Designs and Patents Act, 1988.

Counterpoint Books are available at special discounts for bulk purchases in
the United States by corporations, institutions, and other organizations. For
more information, please contact the Special Markets Department at the
Perseus Books Group, 11 Cambridge Center, Cambridge, MA 02142, or
call (617) 252-5298, (800) 255-1514 or e-mail
special.markets@perseusbooks.com.

A CIP catalogue record for this book is available from the Library
of Congress.
ISBN 1-58243-223-6 (hc.)
ISBN 1-58243-310-0 (pbk.)

Typeset by M Rules
04 05 06 / 10 9 8 7 6 5 4 3 2 1

SCHOPENHAUER'S
TELESCOPE

for Mary

What is your substance, whereof are you made,
That millions of strange shadows on you tend?

WILLIAM SHAKESPEARE

SCHOPENHAUER'S
TELESCOPE

PART I

Noon

On the Way to the Field

As often happens when snow falls, the morning was mild, but around eleven the wind picked up, snow and ice fell together, and the temperature went below zero. Even though they gave me no time to bring anything with me when they came, I regretted I didn't grab my cap with the furry ear-flaps that hung from the coat hanger by the front door. Simple: just grab, it would have taken a second. Now my ears were sore and swollen and I had all the seconds in the world to feel it.

The snow fell heavier as noon approached. It stuck to the track that led to the field as I marched in front of another man and two soldiers. We slogged along as if we were out for a walk on a winter's day, and our boots sliced into the snow. I stepped into a hollow, and clumps of it slid down my heel and cold water pooled under the arch of my foot. We passed under pine trees that showed green under the branches like coloured light under a white lampshade. I suppose I could say it was a beautiful day, but we said nothing to each other.

The man caught up with me, lit a match and then his cigarette, quickly returned his free hand to his coat pocket and hunched his shoulders as he pulled the cigarette until it glowed.

My ears went numb, but that numbness hurt somehow and penetrated into my spirit; I felt lifeless. The crunch of steps could have been my heart. I looked back at the soldiers. Three steps behind. I thought I might make a run for it. Leave the whole mess behind me and reach the forest and then freedom. Frozen air ballooned from my lips as I took deep breaths and prepared myself. My feet, however, refused to move faster. My legs shook.

I wouldn't make it, anyway. They'd see me make the break, snap out of their own misery, unsling their guns and spray fire until I dropped to the snow and leaked onto it and died.

This far north, sometimes days can't lift themselves above the horizon, can't get down to the door and open it for the sun to shine in. Since dawn very little extra light had filtered down through the clouds, though the snow reflected what light there was. I thought how the time of day seemed perfectly disguised. Twilight? Dawn? Noon? Some days don't ever get going at all.

The field was about a hundred yards ahead. I knew it well, I played there as a child. Eleven acres of flat grass, a small farmhouse, and a barn in one corner that used to house two ponies. The owner was dead, the property claimed in back-taxes by the town. A pine forest bordered on three sides; on the fourth, a wall ran alongside the track. I smelled the forest, tasted the sharp tang of bark on the air.

As we passed the first of two gates into the field, I heard a mumble and looked around. One of the soldiers had raised a hand and I glanced to where he pointed; I nodded, trudged over to the second gate, and waited as the man stood to one side. The younger soldier swung it open and motioned me in.

We entered the field, I first, the man behind me, the soldiers behind him. The soldiers sat down behind a gun emplacement. The man and I crossed to the middle of the field to a section where the snow dipped about a metre deep in a rectangular cut, about six metres by two. I knew when the man stopped half way to the hole because his boots no longer crunched in the snow. The next part of the journey was mine alone.

I looked up at a pickaxe as it flew through the air. It landed a few feet ahead of me. One of the soldiers threw a shovel that dropped and skidded between us. I picked it up and walked to the edge of the depression, took a deep breath, looked around me once more, and stepped in.

THE HOLE

I grew up in sight of this field. I played here as a child on my way home from school, though usually on my own, because I was never that popular, for reasons I now understand. My impulse was to be alone, and by my sixteenth year I no longer played with the other schoolboys at all, not even football, not even in warm weather. Instead, I read books over there by the wall or under that tree. The field inclined from south to north so that in rainy times a pool gathered at the south end where in autumn migrating geese landed to rest. They cackled so much the field itself seemed alive. In summer, the ground softened under rain and felt like brown flesh with grass for skin, perfumed with all the flowers that found their way through the surface. In winter it was a hard field, not made of flesh at all, not made of anything except the hardness that stops your boot from sinking for ever into the snow, a hardness that says, *Ground*.

I took the shovel and heaved to the side the snow that had fallen on the partially dug hole, all under the disinterested gaze of the man who stood six metres away. He plucked another cigarette from a silver case, tapped it, and placed it between his lips, never took his eyes off me, his left hand snug in his pocket.

————

Hardly a day for momentous events, and anything written in the book of history about today would be erased by fat grey clouds that shed cold crystals everywhere and anywhere, on the pine trees, on the lights and spires of the town visible a mile away in the dim morning light. This was a day to hide things in. The gusty wind found every footprint and filled it, along with its direction, and our presence in the field would leave little impression and even less evidence. In fact, that November 25th offered nothing to the senses to distinguish it from any other winter day in earth's rotation and the rotation of air through every pair of lungs or under every pair of wings. But it's well known that all events have to occur in a day of some kind.

Although a baker by trade, today I was a digger. I shovelled for maybe twenty minutes and alternated with the pickaxe to loosen the hard clay. A good rhythm. The man went through three cigarettes. In no hurry, I scraped a thin film of snow with each swing and spread it wide in the air to give the illusion of volume and so keep myself busy longer. After I hit clay I did the same. The man made no move to correct my method, if he did notice anything. With each upward movement I took stock of my surroundings. A tractor with mud frozen on its wheels stood in the doorway of the barn, along with forks that hung from the beam, and the stable for the ponies that hadn't been seen since the day before yesterday, when the soldiers first came to the town. Snow on the barn roof, on the fence that circled the barn, dropping off the branches in the rising wind.

I shovelled to keep warm, to keep my heart beating, yes, my heart beating. I repeated these words in time with my dig and swing: *Ice and snow, wind. Ice and snow, wind. Stay alive. Stay alive.*

We were in the middle of nowhere, we had a baby blizzard growing bigger, and, despite my attempts at delay, I was already a metre down into the hole.

When Genial Men Come

It's remarkable how quickly you can get into trouble.

The war had come to our town and left it in the space of two days. Some smoke still rose from shelled-out buildings in the town; otherwise a vast silence lingered in the air. The battle sounds of the days before had grown distant. I guessed that our neighbours in the next town, fifteen kilometres down the road, must be in the middle of it now. They'd die like most people do, in a panic, one hand on their children, the other to their god, if they believed in one, or in a fight to the end if they didn't.

After the fast battle for the town had ended, and the blackened soldiers had moved on or been put in hospital or buried, I noticed a new breed of men filter from the main approach road into the town streets. They wore pullovers and caps, and one of them even smoked a pipe. Could have been a hunting party or a golf crew. A few at first, they went through the town pointing at important buildings and getting in and out of nondescript cars. Then some hours passed and more came in, better dressed. They set up headquarters in the beer hall. These men were genial. I heard they liked wine and dined at the local restaurant. With a detachment of green-uniformed soldiers following them in jeeps and on foot, they went through the town's records, consulted tax documents, property lists.

By eight o'clock that evening, they had drawn up a different kind of list, written, I was told, in pencil and in capitals. My name must have been near the top of that list, because they came to my house that night, directly from the beer hall.

THE TEACHER

When I noticed him, it was too late. The man almost on top of me. Caught me off guard as I dug. He walked up to the edge and looked into the hole in the winter field, not far from thick woods and a wall that trailed like a child's aimless scribble across the cold blade of that November day.

I let the shovel drop and spat a piece of glass onto my gloves and rubbed them uselessly together for a little warmth, as I'd often done on chilly spring mornings when I was still the town baker and I eased the door shut behind me as dawn rose above the rooftops behind my bakery. There, I could work in peace among the empty ovens lined up for the poultices of flour and water and oil, on my own, the way I was used to. I could work in peace then because I was noticed less than I was now.

My hands froze to the shovel. Nothing could warm my fingers now, not even fire, I thought. I looked at him with a sideways swipe of the eyes then, since he made no effort to greet me or shake my hand, just stood at the hole. His long coat fit him, herringbone tweed perhaps, but too thin for this type of weather, the hat expensive, made to measure, I suspected. His glove drew out yet another cigarette from a silver box he flipped open expertly.

Those things would kill him.

I struck a match for him inside his cupped hands and then lit mine. The stubble on his hard jaw worked as he sucked deep into his lungs. Our eyes met through the smoke.

I have always presumed that a well-dressed person is educated. Look in any clothes shop, any library. One chooses and then wears garments as wisely as one selects a book and reads the words. A cotton shirt, ironed smooth, should lead the eye down to good tweed trousers, just as a crafted and cut sentence blends into a second thought as it finishes with the material of the first.

I read a lot, you see. You learn to do that when you have no friends. It hurts at first, but books never let you down. I have learned a lot from books. This man had yet to speak a word, but he had the gait of learning about him. The educated can be silent better than most. I hate that in them. The young schoolboy in me always wants to talk them into oblivion with all the words I've mastered and can say, just so I can be alone.

I eyed him some more for the one detail that would give him away. Yes, now that I examined him properly, I was fairly certain I'd seen him in town. Yes, many times, though he'd taken better care of himself then. Something about the way he stood. Now I was sure I knew him, even though his face did not register. I puffed at my cigarette. (I have learned to be silent at times like this. Let the other fellow make the first move, that's what I say. I've often regretted making the first move, and that's a fact.)

Finally, he pointed his cigarette at the hole and said, 'Are you finished with that?'

I looked at my feet, where he was pointing.

'Finished with what? What?'

'The hole. Are you done with it?'

He shivered and drew his collar up and took another pull. I stared at the hole and then I took a step toward him. He had asked a good question, to the point but not simplistic. He glanced at the shovel spotted with snowflakes.

Closer. I knew him.

'I'll bet you're the teacher, the history teacher,' I said.

'Correct.' He snapped a smile at me and arched one eyebrow. 'The hole?'

'That's a good question,' I said. 'Of course you would ask, being a teacher. When is one ever finished with a hole?'

I took the shovel and slammed it against a rock to crack the ice off it. The teacher did not flinch. I suspected he didn't like me, thought I was above my station because I talked to him like that instead of a quick answer and a tip of my hat in politeness to my better and superior fellow citizen. But it was too cold a morning for that, and I'd dug hard, outpaced a sky full of relentless snow with a gang of clouds lined up all the way to the rim of as far as I could see. Sorry, no civility today, come back tomorrow and we'll see. He sensed my anger and must have felt sorry, or sorry for me, because he spoke again in a softer tone.

'Digging a hole on a day like this, you might as well plug a dam with peanuts,' he said. 'It can't be done. Today you are Sisyphus.'

I stepped out and took his second shuffle of a cigarette. He gazed into the hole and seemed to measure it with puffs of smoke, tracing a finger around its dimensions until he came to the mound of white-capped clay to the side. He was a man of many thoughts, buried in his subject. He had taught my brother at the local school, and my brother often came home and told me the stories the somewhat nervous teacher told his students to prove his theory that all history was a cycle. Despite the brutal cold, I wanted to ask the teacher now what sissy pus was, whether a condition of some sort, or an honorary title. It didn't ring well. It sounded like a disease, an appearance of something on the skin, a wound. And I didn't like the way he just threw the word out, as if I was supposed to know these things, a little riddle in the middle of a snowstorm. He made my answer into a needle to stick me with. I took the shovel and jumped into the hole and hacked away at the ground for a clever answer to stab into his jugular. My digging had put me at eye level with his thighs. He made no attempt to move as I swung at the ground like a pendulum.

I had read once in a science book that when you are anxious you can see better out of the sides of the eyes than straight ahead. You can't read well when you are anxious for that reason. The body has learned through countless ambushes that attacks usually come from the side, the trees, the high grass. How true: the shovel and the pickaxe were just a blur in front of me as my sense of sight pooled its resources in the corners of my vision, and I observed the rhythm of his breath shimmy up in ropes from his parted lips, a cold sore on the lower, and observed it with remarkable clarity.

He kicked at the snow.

'So, my friend. Here we are, you and I. Yes, indeed. It's a fine hole you've dug. I'm sure the pre-Socratics would solve our problem of the hole.'

He looked down at me and said, 'The philosophers. You know of them? Theories of construction of the universe?'

My heart pounded, but I answered without delay. 'I am a baker. I construct loaves. Talk a language I can understand.' It was a knee-jerk reaction, to blurt out a wisecrack. It came out even though I didn't mean to say it. I was a schoolboy again, being taunted and whispered about, and now, as then, I snapped when I was vulnerable. True, I was frightened, but my best choice was to act smart and clever, as if I wasn't afraid. They'd respect that, me not giving an inch.

He continued, 'Well, look at it this way. Is the hole the space you've dug or is it made of the clay and snow you've dug out?'

I shovelled faster, a boil of nonchalance.

His cigarette traced the red line of his thoughts in the air.

'Nietzsche nailed it, of course. Real philosophical enquiry died with the arrival of Plato.'

I pressed the shovel blade with my foot. 'Why?'

'Because,' he said, 'Plato said the answers lay elsewhere, in the heavens. Don't trust what you see. That was the beginning of the great lie.' He chuckled. 'It's obvious. And then you have heaven, which is nothing but a hole in our thinking.'

He made an arc with his arms and I saw his neck veins bulge as he looked up into the snow-laden sky. 'Look at it,' he said. 'Ridiculous, a place full of angels and a little honey and milk. Isn't that the biblical description? What a hell of a place to spend eternity.'

I thought then that he might be delusional. It was one of those sudden thoughts that crop up in the mind and you don't know where they come from, how far back into the memory of time and survival. But you learn to listen to them. *Oh yes you do.*

He gripped his coat, caught in a fierce surge of wind like

a thousand thrown knives. I ducked and the hole protected me; the gust blew over my head.

'How far are we from town?' he shouted into the wind. 'I've lost my bearings in this mess.' His words chattered.

'A little over a kilometre, same as it always was.' No going back now.

Wrapped in the coat, he composed himself and beat his sides with his fists. He smiled and said, 'Do you know that early medieval man lived most of his life within a day's journey of his village? Did you know that?'

I dug deeper and shafted mud and ice in huge thrusts. Now that this man had warmed up to himself, I was probably in for an earful.

'Such forests everywhere,' he said. 'Villagers got lost easily. And if they went off to war, and survived it, they often failed to find their home afterwards. Hundreds, thousands of men, gone astray in the dark. It was a fact of life.'

I stabbed a difficult root. 'Your point?' I said.

'I am practically lost here, in the place I grew up,' he said, and glanced around in a shiver, 'and I'm sure I could see my chimney stack if the day were clear. Imagine if this were all dense forest. No sun, no paths but a few trails for hundreds of kilometres. That was Europe. Most hardly knew what decade it was, let alone the time of day. But I grew up in this town. I should really know where I am.'

'Will there be a test after this?' I asked. 'A sort of history test?'

He laughed and stooped to clap me on the back. I flinched at the intimacy.

'Very good. No test, not today. Keep digging, if you will.'

'I will.'

And I did. I had talked back, and I was still alive.

THE BATTLE

Two days ago the war came to our town.

The border tension turned into a skirmish and then, inevitably, a battle, and, of course, a war. You can set your watch by human conflict. It matches self-interest to the nearest second.

For a week the shooting stayed at the border. Reports from there suggested an even match and a possible deal. But the fight wouldn't quit. I could hear it from my bedroom, rumbles, the odd flash across the wall. I woke one night when the background noise became foreground noise, the gunfire definitely louder, probably on the approach road to us from the border town. Must have been a breakthrough. Our people couldn't hold them.

Then the explosions. The ground shivered.

It was barely daylight. I got out of bed and crawled on my belly to the window and put my eye in one corner. My heart locked in fear and thumped to free itself from my blood. Instead of a rhythmical de-dump, de-dump, it said, *Get out, get out.*

The gunfire got louder, then went through the roof, and the war introduced itself with barely so much as a nod. First soldiers in black uniforms, the defenders, ran through town with as many guns as they could carry. The skirmish lasted five, ten minutes at most. The soldiers in black retreated too fast to defend the town. Surprised by an assault, probably.

They ran and turned, fired a shot. Ran and turned, fired a shot. Clearly hadn't been able to establish a position. And this: how metallic the guns sounded! The whole event was heat and steel and no human sounds at all, it seemed to me. Nothing like that. Might well have been robots fighting. Screams, shouts, not a thing. Cordite, oil, the smell of cabbage from an upturned bin on the road where a cat froze between eating and fleeing and ran into the bin when bullets ricocheted around the street in a furious tap dance of erupting sparks. That's all I heard of anyone. Shadows ran, flames darted from the dark like blowtorches.

Then a sound like an organ grinder bashing empty cans. A tank.

It clanked around the corner and braked shrilly in the town square. The engine rumbled my house to its foundations. What a terrible sound, that rumble. My house was paper, my skin water, my life transparent all of a sudden. I thought, *I am going to die.*

They kill everyone, you know.

The black uniforms turned and shot at the tank but the tracers glanced off the hull and scored the houses instead. The tank's gun creaked higher and spat yellow smoke: two hundred yards away a tower lost its upper third in a dull brown explosion of brick. The turret swung, the forward machine gun fired in short bursts. And then around the tank, as if given birth from it, men filed in green uniforms. Their guns blazed at the black uniforms. One of the attackers stayed in the open instead of along walls and houses, confident perhaps because of the tank, but a tracer cut him to a hop and he let go of his gun, knelt on both knees, fell forward into the mud, and did not move.

And like a spring rain shower, the fight passed through the town. The metallic blasts faded, hollower, thinner. Then silence for an hour or so. No one dared come out onto the streets. The sun rose. Then more soldiers in green uniforms arrived in trucks, better dressed, less battle-weary – or maybe they looked better because the light made their skin fleshier. Less like ghosts. Of course, they were alive and the sun shone. No one looks like a ghost in those conditions. And when the sun was higher I saw three more dead, one with his leg stuck in the air and his foot hanging by an ankle ligament. The other two could have been snoozing after a day at the harvest. I was mildly disappointed at the sight of my first battle dead.

The green soldiers wasted no time. House to house, evicted everyone.

They came for me too.

WINTER

One thing you learn about deep cold, it has a cousin called silence that follows it in the door whenever it comes to visit. Even the strike of a shovel against stones doesn't long survive cold. Nothing does. Your breath is caught and frozen in flight, your speech splits open a second out of the throat, your words break in the cocoon of your sentences.

As the brutal wind whipped across the field, my head went down and my mouth shut tight. My lips pressed against each other with a cold blue tongue between them. The snow laid itself across my shoulders, drifted in my lungs, inches of it on my heart, metres of it on my eyes, knives of it between my toes, hells of it in my pores, rivers of its icy melt down my sweaty back.

Like the perfect parasite, snow is a genius of obstruction, a firm pressure against your will; no matter how balanced your temperament when you set out on your journey, it bullies away your resistance, gets you swearing. Sucks your energy away through the soles of your boots. That's winter here. It will not be ignored. Not fought with. Not chased away with sticks. It comes in late October, baring teeth. You bow before it for five months. It leaves. You recover.

That's my philosophy of winter.

THE TEACHER'S LEFT HAND

For obvious reasons, I had kept a close eye on the teacher's left hand. When he lifted it out of his pocket I expected some sort of handgun, an antique one as a kind of gesture, a derringer, a Webley, a Mauser. Nothing of the sort. The cigarette hand moved from his mouth and his delicate left hand tipped a hip flask to his lips. He raised it to me in salute.

'Good whisky.'

The pickaxe glanced sparks off a stone and gouged the packed clay.

I said, 'I don't drink.'

He smiled, 'Don't know what you're missing.'

'What time is it?' I asked.

'You've dug for thirty-five, forty minutes. That makes it about twelve forty.'

Left hand back in the pocket. *What else was in there?*

'Do you want some water?'

I ignored him. That way he couldn't lord it over me with any more questions. Besides, I faced a logistical problem with the hole. At just over a metre deep, I needed to widen it as well as dig deeper. Should I dig all the way down in one place first and then widen it? That way I'd be out of the wind for a while. After some thought I decided to widen it and work my way down evenly. This would keep my swings steady and even and keep my eyes longer on the teacher and the soldiers behind him.

If it came, I wanted to look it in the eye.

At around one o'clock, the sky darkened. The hole was no deeper, but I had achieved the correct length and width and besides built a nice wind block around the hole with the clay and snow on one side.

The teacher, who had never left his spot by the hole, asked me if I wanted a break.

'Would you like to talk about why you're here?' he said.

I didn't fall for that one. No confessions, no heart-to-heart, man-to-man exchanges.

'You know it'll get worse,' he said.

I froze.

He said, 'I mean the weather. We could be here another couple of hours, and we should really talk while you work.'

He shifted his head in the direction of the soldiers at the gun emplacement.

'Those two wouldn't be much company for me. You, on the other hand, must have quite a lot to say that would be of great interest to me.'

I said, without looking up, 'I am a baker by trade. We can talk the bakery trade if you like. I wouldn't have much else to say to you or anyone else.'

He didn't like that and retreated a few steps, turned his back. And then, if you can possibly believe this, the wind changed direction and cold air swept under a black cloud. I cursed it, cursed the useless wind block, and dug faster, shivered and sweated at the same time. I was now in a race with the weather and with my enemies, and the only way to buy time was to dig myself deeper into a hole in the ground.

THE CITY

I cut the next layer of earth out with the pickaxe. This far down I found rocks I couldn't split, so I pried them loose first and then shovelled them or threw them over the top. No help from the teacher; he sat himself down on one of the bigger rocks I heaved up. Lit another cigarette, of course. *Did the man have lungs left at all?*

As I worked, I remembered that my brother, when a student in the teacher's class at the local school, often complained at home about the intense man with the big stories and the strange theories, the massive amount the teacher required them to read, the speeches they had to give pretending they were this or that leader.

He even made them read classical Latin poetry and medieval war epics, said if he had his way that everyone would learn how to fence and play chess, said that poetry was as much a part of history as facts and dates ever were. Well, according to my brother, the teacher was the only one in the school who talked like that. Even his colleagues said he was 'a bit different, but that's okay.'

Now this same man looked down at me in a hole on the deserted edges of town. It was a harder day than it needed to be.

———

My brother said that one morning the teacher walked into the classroom and announced, 'It is the thirteenth of February.'

But it was not the thirteenth, and not February. He walked into class in the month of October. No one had a clue what he was talking about. Eight months off with his date. My brother said the teacher spoke in a strange tone, and what happened next is mostly what my brother related to me. The rest I put together to keep my mind occupied while I swung the snow and dirt away from me.

(Know thine enemy. *And if you can't know him, imagine him.*)

'Today is the thirteenth of February,' the teacher said, and placed his briefcase on the table. 'And on this date, a war has twelve weeks left to run. The place, a medieval city undefended, a place of parks, a zoo, a choir, dolls, and china, famed for its architecture. The city produces china, and its nineteen hospitals house the war wounded. The city has no military value. The city's men are away fighting at the front. The lesson, saturation precision bombardment. I will use three breaths only, one for each wave of bombers.'

Three breaths? The whisper went round the class. He'd lost his mind. Maybe some boys should run to the office and tell the headmaster that the history teacher wanted to choke himself. A pillow over the head without the pillow. Suicide by talking. In silence behind their rows of desks, they sat and waited. (I have learned that most bystanders do nothing anyway in an emergency.)

Standing at the head of the class, the teacher closed his eyes.

'I will speak initially only for as long as one breath lasts, since those not burned in the city suffocated, and today we must relive that in their memory, to know what it is to asphyxiate.'

My brother said he caught himself holding his breath, trying to imagine how bad it was, could hold it only seconds because his heart was beating too fast, let it go, tried to last with his breath out, gave up fast, and hoped no one saw him do it.

On that morning in class, the teacher closed his eyes and took deep draughts and droned. My brother remembers most of it because he was in the front row: the drone was like aircraft, he said, and the drone was like words that hadn't formed yet. The boys wondered what was next, sat uneasily in their rows of seats, and the pressure of the teacher's steady monotone got to them. Then the drone formed into words, and he spoke faster, every word part of the drone and yet every word separate and clear.

'Women, children, over a million people, half of them refugees from the east fleeing the Russians, reported to be only ninety-five kilometres from the city. The train station filled with refugees, people sleeping on the freezing streets, suffering from stress and hunger. Because it was Shrove Tuesday, a few girls paraded in costume, and the circus played to a full house. People walked in the great park.

'The attackers' plan was to land incendiary bombs in tight sectors across the city, ignite hundreds of fires at strategic points. In theory, the fires would rush together and incinerate the city. The first wave, which arrived shortly after 10:00 p.m., consisted of two hundred and fifty bombers. The second wave brought five hundred bombers a few hours later, catching the firefighters and survivors in the open. The third wave of two hundred Flying Fortresses appeared at 11:30 a.m. the following morning, accompanied by fighters that strafed the roads around the city. Now I will begin.'

'We thought you already had,' someone said.

The teacher took a deep breath.

'Fighter planes marked the city with green flares. Bombs fell on the train station, burned three thousand people. Bombs crashed into the circus. Timber houses in the old town caught fire, and the blistering air whirled into a violent updraft. A firestorm was born – so intense that it whipped any available oxygen into itself, vacuuming cars and buildings and trees and anything loose into the flames. Women's bellies tore open with the compression and the unborn burst out of them. People tore off their burning clothes in the streets, passed out from lack of oxygen, and then caught fire, shrunk to cinders the size of babies.'

My brother says that even the tough boys swallowed as they listened to the strained voice of the teacher dredge the end of that first breath.

'The second wave viewed the city from eighty kilometres away, a scorch in the night sky. The bombers flew in so low that the crews could see people's faces in the streets, and they saw some of them flying through the air, screaming, into the fires. The bombers released their payload, starting hundreds of small fires. Sucked by the firestorm at the centre, the small fires converged across the city. In the cellars, people boiled and turned to liquid. In the great park, the flames raced across the grass and consumed thousands who took shelter there.'

At that point, the teacher paused, breathed rapidly, inhaled, and held it.

'When the second wave was done, those still alive in the cellars suffocated because the firestorm removed all the oxygen from the air. Those who ran into the street couldn't breathe. Some screamed as the howling furnace pulled them off their feet and into the inferno. High above, the planes gyrated on the unstable air as the crews shielded their eyes. Far down, in the hell of the city, a zoo blazed. Terrified and in agony, apes, bison, and red buffalo escaped. They ran alongside the residents who fled the flames, attacking some. The vultures flew to safety, spreading out over the city, but the following morning settled around the zoo grounds, because it was their feeding time.'

The boys agreed that the teacher had breathed more than once for the second wave. They could not see how he did it otherwise. But they discussed that later, much later. For now, they said nothing. The blood had quit their faces.

The teacher leaned on a desk and stared at the floor, heaving in air.

'Hospital authorities dragged surviving patients to the river and lay them along the banks. The third wave caught them, and fighters strafed the wounded in the park and on the roads leading out of the city, killing thousands. They strafed the zoo and killed the remaining animals. People ran, gone mad, their hair on fire. One hundred and thirty-five thousand killed and I can't . . .'

My brother said the teacher's face turned blue and his eyes bulged. He collapsed forward, gasped over his books, a strangled despair on his face. He sucked the air into him like a cold drink of water. He looked up.

'They say one hundred and fifty thousand. Maybe more.'

Silence. Everyone held his breath. Silence. Like the sound the dead make. Someone said later, 'Yeah, quieter than silence.' Someone laughed in a shriek. The teacher took his bags and left the classroom without another word or glance at anyone.

The next day he wrote on the board, THEY PRAYED TO GOD IN THE CITY, BUT THE DEVIL ANSWERED. 'Write a 500 word essay.'

I dug.

My brother came home and said that the people in that city must have lived more than three breaths, so on that count alone the teacher was wrong. And he cheated on the count, anyway. My brother also said that the teacher never lived in that city, and what if a few animals and some people died? It was war, and things happened in war. We all agreed. War is war. Most killing, ordinary. If it happened enough, you'd get used to it, wouldn't stop you eating a good breakfast after a while.

I dug.

INFORMATION

'It's one-fifteen,' the teacher said, and changed his position on the rock. He puffed on number five.

'I didn't ask you what time it was.'

'You don't look like you've gone any deeper in fifteen minutes,' he pointed to his watch, 'and I haven't got the entire day. It's dark soon after three. You need to be done by three.'

'Thank you for telling me what I already know.'

'You have to be done before three.'

'I'll be done, don't you worry,' I said.

He said, 'Baker, I'm not worried. I've got nothing to hide.'

That one caught me. Fair enough. As long as he didn't think I was stupid just because he was a teacher and me a baker. The worst thing a person can do is underestimate me. People have done that and I'm still here.

The town I live in is one of many spread out over this peninsula that in winter faces a cold expanse of slate-grey breakers and in summer a turquoise ocean. The biggest town, a few miles to the north, fronts the coast with its ports and loud gulls. It's chilly there even in July, slimy with seaweed on the brilliant blue brine that northern latitude brings. Nobody swims even in a hot summer because a nuclear station used to operate sixty-five kilometres away and got shut down. In the shallow but wide valley of our town, the sun warms the air better. You can taste the sea on the wind in a hot green field.

In winter, though, you're on your own.

I learned that as a young boy. I also learned that you're on your own not just in winter. You're on your own in everything. At school, everyone seemed to know more than I did. Knew people I didn't know. Better families than mine. Damned from birth, I was. Left out at crucial moments at playtime, in discussions at class. Comments about the way I talked, my appearance. I guessed then there was more of the same to come.

That's when I discovered friends a little bit older and a lot wiser than my mates at school. These friends lived between covers in the library, and most had some very interesting information to share with me. Helped me get ahead. They asked me not to divulge the fact that I had all this information. Well, they didn't ask, but that's the way I see it. My books were my best and only friends. I just kept my head down, minded my own business, and waited for my chance to put what I'd read into action.

One chance came a week after my twentieth birthday. But first, a lot of people one day might want to know how I came to know so much. The reason? I needed to be certain about things, as many things as I could be certain about. No more doubt.

Down in the hole, I occupied myself with how I came to know so much about so many things.

My climb to certainty came from not knowing anything at all. I was the last one to get a clever joke, a quick reference;

I was the one who laughed because everyone else did. Nervous of groups, I had to drag myself to even the most informal night at a bar. I nodded when everyone else agreed. I shook my head and made a suitable noise when the company expressed disapproval. I lived in fear of being asked my opinion first, before I was able to get the measure of everyone else's, in terror of being the yardstick, in shame of my sure silence while people waited for my response.

But my books helped me. I gained the insights of all outsiders: I understood how power worked. Power grew not in leaps but in small steps, skips and turns. How local boys no more clever than I mentioned the right names at employment interviews, saluted unimportant people at the right time, reached a hand across a crowd and shook a significant hand. I saw how some women attached themselves to certain men, sometimes because a man had a good job, sometimes because he ignored her.

I bought a good dictionary and learned the science of phonetics, so that I could speak without an accent, be a citizen of no country and every country. I went to the library and rented music, Brandenburg Concertos, Water Music, Finlandia, conducted them in my bathroom, corrected minor blemishes as the loudspeakers boomed from the tub for better acoustics. I read a history of inventions. I consumed the generals and their victories, their losses. I studied *The Art of War*. How to win in battle, how to run from a hopeless fight.

And the months and then the years went on, until after a lot of learning, I made a huge decision. I decided that I no longer knew nothing about anything; on the contrary, I resolved to use other words to describe my knowledge: *maybe, perhaps, sometimes*. I read that very smart people preferred those words. So I used them. I now thought that *maybe* I was the only one in town unloved by women. That *maybe* those boys laughed at me. That *perhaps* fate had left me to discover my own devices at school and at home, left me to discover like a loose cub in the wild how indifferent the world is when you bring little it can use. Not pretty, not clever, no important daddy. I thought maybes, mights, and possibles. (I let few objects escape the grip of the conditional, which is a word, a time verb, which I found out about by reading.)

I still attended church by my early teens, though when others read or sang I weighed the question of god, and surmised that yes, God probably existed; otherwise why would all these people sit here? No one could fool this many! And when the boys I would soon part ways with when school ended stared blankly ahead and thought of girls, I stared at the timber with the man on it and surmised that cruelty was perhaps a fact of life. *Relax, relax*, I said to myself. I read somewhere, I'm sure, that you must learn to soften the muscles that make you frown, yes, soften, but retain the determination to get beyond that to a posture that benefits you. I read more. I saw the patterns of history and thought that a human might be eighty per cent chemicals, eighteen per cent his past, and two per cent feeling, creatures of habit. Which makes psychiatrists really pharmacists who have to listen longer.

But I had so much to learn about what made people work.

I often thought that my distance from everyone came from inside. I stood at the edge of the fog around me, I watched the people of the world enjoy life and wondered how I could make my way to that place through the plastic that allowed me to see but not touch, or touch but with this crinkly substance between my skin and the brightest sunshine, the widest smile, the deepest blue, the shiniest pear, the sweetest voice, sharpest pinprick, briefest moment, soundest sleep. Ordinary joy is what you might call it, laughter, ease, those kinds of words and all the other ones that you might employ in a list that contained those kinds of words.

And one fine day, as I walked alone to work, I thought that I might possibly use people and so protect myself. I placed this thought in a special place in my mind and fed it every day.

Can't move much when you've got that clear plastic all over you like an umbrella. Got to figure out the way they move. Time them with a watch. Like the mother lion shows the young ones how to chase and eat. How many steps to coffee, to get a job, to manage a loan, to throw bread to pigeons, to wash a car, to stroll alone round the town square on a Saturday morning during farmers' market, nodding with hands joined behind the back. To learn how humans walk and talk.

Citizen watch, that's what I called myself. *Now watch, citizens.*

I learned yoga from a book, took air deep into my belly and only then let my chest expand. I learned positions with great care, one per month. Strange how your body twists into a shape and you change the way you think; makes you more efficient. I drank yoga instead of beer because it gave me control. I filled my stomach with air, let all the tension drain out of my head with all of my opinions, let the air all sink down into my guts. Don't mind a puffy belly. Good to stretch the guts, get things moved around the pipes a bit. Don't stick your chest out because there's little to stretch there. But the names of the poses were so long. Too hard to pronounce. Maybe there's a posture for the mouth that happens when you say the name of the posture. *Vala* something something or *Tukandra*. *Vindra* extrasyllableshere. (What is a mouth anyway? Is it the tongue, the gums, the teeth, the lips, the plates or whatever they are above and beneath? And another question: What is a mouth?)

I prefer the Western names for yoga postures better, like *The Cobra*. Yes, lie on your stomach, place your hands under your shoulders, arch the back up, lean lightly on the thighs, arch the head back. And bite! Yeah, bite anyone who comes near. That's my philosophy of life. If they get close, cut them back, kick them back down the ladder. Stab 'em in the back and smile from the front. Now. Where am I? Where was I? What pose was I talking about?

People poses, that's what I learned. I became a person by copying people. When people were happy I noticed they pulled their lips aside and bared their teeth; but I also observed that bared teeth was rage too. I solved this problem. I noted the condition of the eyes and, even more importantly, mimicked any gestures very precisely, like shaking hands or embraces (all in my room, of course; I never touched anyone). The phrases people used were often the same words in mostly the same order. I committed all to memory. *Hello. How are you? Hello, darling. See you tomorrow. Lovely to see you. How are you doing? How are the children? How is the job? Did you hear that so-and-so died/got married/had a child/has moved? You look well/tired/worried/happy/relaxed.*

As I practised these, I became aware that the person I spoke to seemed more relaxed than when I was myself (mostly silent with a scowl or just a blank stare). People seemed to seek out my company more. The conclusion was inevitable: I was a better human now, better at being one.

I learned that everyone learns what he knows by copying. There's not one skill that he doesn't copy. His mother teaches him to walk, to talk, to eat, the school teaches him to write by imitation, to read by imitation, the elders teach him to believe what the truth is, what it looks like, where he can find it, and what to do with it. Yellow is something on the skin of a banana. He learns hot by touch, soft by touch. Sex, he reads about that or catches his parents at it or spies on the next-door neighbours. Monkey see, monkey do. He learns that the future is behind and the past in front, rather than the other way around, because he can't see the future with his eyes. But the past is visible because it has happened, so it's in front.

My list of knowledges grew. I proceeded to more certain words, such as *every, always, all*. Every war is lost by both sides. Every person will always act in his own interest at all times. All wars begin with people who have something to gain. Every love affair begins with self-interest and ends the same. I made these types of statements privately, of course, usually in my bedroom or in my mind, because of the border conflict: you spoke with an unspoken fear of being on the wrong side if things went bad.

And things always go bad.

In the days when the conflict confined itself to the border, the fighting was mostly stray shots over the fences, an artillery shell that popped yellow stuff that some said was chemical. Denials everywhere. Politicians with neckties shook heads on camera and pointed to agreements. Then the shooting got worse and people realized that they might die. By the time the town's morale deteriorated into possibles and probables and uncertainties, I had graduated to certainty. I knew where I should stand on all issues.

I wasn't going to stand in the crowd.

THE BAKER'S APPRENTICE

My life changed shortly after my twentieth birthday when I answered a notice for a baker's apprentice written in bad handwriting on the window of a local shop. The man at the counter looked too old to be working. Round glasses, round face, round belly, round head.

'Hello,' he said with a round smile. 'What can I get you?'

'The apprentice job,' I said, pointing to the window.

He moved to the side of the counter, held out a big round hand to shake mine, and said, 'But aren't you a bit – a bit grown up for that?'

'Is the job open?'

'Yes,' he said. 'And I'd love you to work here, yes, of course.' And he took out a big round cigar and lit it with a fat flame.

A girl came out of the back room where I guessed the baking was done and placed fresh loaves on the counter. Quiet, my age. She smiled at me too. I shifted my gaze because I don't like looking people in the eyes. The old baker took her by the shoulder and said, 'This is my daughter. This place will be hers one day.'

Her teeth were as white as the flour under his nails.

———

I came back the next day. At least, I began watching the old baker, because that's all he let me do. He repeated the words, 'Watch and learn, watch and learn, drink tea, relax.' He was a careful baker, I'll give him that.

After the first weeks, when the old man let me watch but not touch anything, he finally allowed me to prepare the dough. Under his gaze and occasional corrective finger, I learned the sponge-and-dough method. He moved slowly, showing me each step many times, saying 'Like this, like this.'

I combined wheat flour, water and yeast into a sponge and added salt to control the rate of fermentation. I placed the dough in a mixer, where the horizontal bars developed its fibres and structure. From there I dumped the lot into the trough, a metal tank, where it proved. The baker taught me that after three to five hours, the 'break' happened, where the dough decreased in volume. Then I learned to return it to the mixer and add in the rest of the ingredients. This was the time-consuming part; all that was left then was to let it ferment some more, shape, and bake the dough.

I learned quickly and won the man's heart. But I never particularly liked him. Too easy with his time. Always leaning on something or other, talking about anything and everything with whomever happened to be within earshot. Photos of his grandchildren. A cigarette outside in the alley every twenty minutes. Sometimes the smell of beer at six in the morning. Clearly not a professional. Not born to it. Didn't really deserve it.

From baking I learned not just certainty but how to create it. I saw that when I combined certain actions and ingredients, the result would be the same every time. From the day the old baker took me in as an apprentice, I committed to memory all the things about baking I saw. At last, at long last: something I could depend on.

His daughter, a quiet girl my age, showed enthusiasm which he rewarded by assigning her on some days the dough preparation, like me, but on other days the mixer, even the baking and handling of hot loaves, which he denied me, despite my hints. But mostly he told her to stay in the front shop and sell to customers who called her by name and sometimes stroked her hair in fond greeting. *If she is behind the counter, she must be okay*, they probably thought. I sensed that I could be the son the baker never had, and I resolved to play that role. It was a sure thing, surely.

I moved out from my parents' house and worked every day assiduously, yes, very assiduously, and lived in a flat above the shop, and I worked very hard for three years until his daughter grew tired of trying to be friendly to me and until the old baker died, surprise surprise, of emphysema. I was nervous about my future since I knew his daughter did not like me. So I was relieved when, on a dry Friday morning, the dead baker's lawyer called.

'I am pleased to inform you that the baker has left instructions that you be retained with responsibilities in all aspects of the baking process, except sales.'

'Except sales?'

'Yes.'

'So I can't be fired.'

'That would be in breach of the stipulations of the will.'

The old baker's daughter took over and was kind to me because her father had requested it.

But she didn't understand the hard side of business. I was not proud of what I did next, but I edged her out over a year and finally made her an offer, four and a half years after I began as an apprentice. She accepted, on the basis of a bank loan I obtained with the condition that I procure ownership of the bakery, although I think she would have liked to remain the owner because the shop contained all her memories of childhood and her father. To save her any further torture, I hooked her up with a man who took her off to another country with some of my borrowed money in his pocket.

On the day they left, I followed them to the bus and watched as it pulled away. She pressed her face to the window until his arm drew her away.

At last, the bakery was mine and no one could take it from me.

I walked taller from that day on. Did not avoid people, did not grovel before the customers. I'd always have a job; people always have to eat. I practised my new importance in front of the mirror in my bedroom. A certain walk. I faced the palms back.

Town baker. Town baker. Yes.

To prepare the grand opening of my bakery, I closed the shop for one day. To get additional customers, I placed a neat banner in the front window detailing cut prices in bakery products for a week. Many people lived near the bread line; ours is not a rich town. Sure enough, new people came who would normally bake their own bread to save a little money, as well as the old reliables, the ones who knew the old baker's daughter by name, who had rarely seen or acknowledged me as I toiled in the dark, hot baking rooms.

Now they all acknowledged me, the short man with the watery eyes. Maybe reluctantly, but they had no choice. The only baker in town. And I watched them too, just as I had watched and learned the trade.

I learned how to read people's movements as their eyes swept the first days' offerings: Vienna breads, maple walnut bread, potato bread, sourdough, rye, pumpkin, fruit, baguettes, apricot nut bread, yeast rolls, wheat bread, raisin bread. Much more variety than the old baker had ever offered. I saw how their eyes bounced off some items and came to rest briefly on others, or returned again and again to items they liked, as they checked the change in their hands or pockets. I adjusted my prices and variety to get them to spend more.

I learned the types of customer: the people who came to buy quickly, the creatures of habitual taste, and those who came to idle, to pass a few minutes in conversation. And I obliged, but always with an eye to the door so that they would never feel completely at home and waste too much of my time. I experimented with the shape of breads: oblong, round, flat. I tried different basic flavours, malty molasses, plain taste, salty. Even the texture proved a challenge because some customers preferred a hard-crust loaf no matter what the ingredients, while others demanded the lighter, doughier type, and still others a coarse-crumb texture.

The truth is that I did very well. I soon made enough money to live in a house in town and employ a helper in the proving room, a lazy schoolboy who had to do because no one else answered the notice for employment I pasted on the front window. He needed money more than his pride. Maybe he got laughed at because he worked for me.

I fired him when he stole from me.

All this success and I was still on my own. There are two ways you can be on your own, that's what I think. You can be the fish in the tank that gets fed, or you can be the hand that sprinkles the food across the surface.

THE FIRST TRUCK

The sky darkened. The sweeps of wind grew longer, the snow thicker, harder. It seemed to me that all the world's winds blew into this field, and from this field, into me.

'You've been very quiet for the last ten minutes,' the teacher said. He stood and kicked his legs straight. 'And working hard, so I'll not complain.'

'I'll work whatever way I want to.'

He smiled. 'Ah, a speech! The Baker has convictions to express.' He addressed an invisible crowd. 'Everybody, down tools while the Baker forms a union.'

Sarcasm didn't suit him. The teacher didn't have the face for it, though it contained the lines of a thousand years of learned history. He apparently chose to keep most of it to himself. A hard man to read, and I didn't like that, and a tough opponent, but experience dictated that he'd soon play his hand. I just had to keep my mouth shut.

Cigarette number six, and his long coat twisted in the storm.

At about one thirty in the afternoon, the sound of a changed gear tore the wind. I worked on, determined not to look. The only way here was along the track we'd come, up a shallow hill, and judging by the numerous gear changes, they had a tough time of it in the weather. Wheels probably spun and the truck skidded, wipers at the fastest speed. The engine noise dimmed as the truck reached the top of the incline. A squeal of brakes, an opened door.

Then I looked, as if I didn't care.

The driver slammed the door and walked casually to the back of the truck that faced the gate, slipped a bolt and pulled down the tailgate, blew into his hands and stepped out of the exhaust fumes. I saw overcoats and long dresses move in the back of the truck. And in those overcoats and long dresses were mostly men and a few children, huddled, freezing, who jumped out or eased themselves down in twos and threes, stretched themselves a little and followed his finger to the oak that towered above the entrance to the field.

They made a strange bunch, the first crew here. Most held rags to their faces or had wrapped them around noses and ears. Men walked at different speeds to the gate, and when they reached it, stood differently, some perfectly still, some leaping and bending to keep warm. Some carried bundles strung from their wrists, others found things to stare at. One jumped from a stationary position, and one, a man in a red hat, drew in the snow with the tip of his shoe, poised like a ballerina. I recognized him as the cobbler, and no doubt that shoe was made of the best leather. I remembered then his last visit to my shop, and I looked for and saw his dog, a skinny spaniel, where it had roped itself into his armpit, its rear angled into the cold, a position he often carried it in as he waited for the apple cakes that dog liked so much, as he told me often enough when he crooned to and sometimes scolded that rear end as he left the shop with the apple cakes his dog liked so much. What a tiresome man! At the bakery I'd watch the dog's face as the man walked out. The ideal customer, that dog, who liked my apple cakes so much. Kept his mouth shut otherwise.

More townspeople shuffled from the truck to the gate: there went the banker. Stood apart under a tree off to the right, maintained a distance from the people who owed him. The clergyman held his little black book in his hand and a good number of the town's indiscretions in his head. The owner of the town cinema watched the event as if it were a spectacle people should pay to watch.

The children found sticks to play with. Always want to play, young children. When they could learn about the world and how it works.

THE MYSTERY OF WHEAT

I looked away and returned to the dig and cursed at the stony ground and the pain in my elbows, worried why I felt nothing from my forearms down. The teacher took another swig from his hip flask, and I noted that my head was now level with his knees.

My heart beat faster. How predictable. How utterly predictable. The teacher came right to the edge of the hole and kicked some snow into it.

'Faster,' he said. 'Can't you see they're here?'

I held the shovel still. Strange how quickly rage can inject itself into your blood and swim around in you like it owns the place.

I raised the shovel an inch. Just an inch. Cradled the handle.

Whenever I've been in a crisis, I've run to my books. I've learned a lot from books, and all of it secretly, and all of it free, experience without having to live it. Someone had to live it and you get the lessons for nothing. Who could turn that deal down? But what could I do now?

Patience. You are the one in the hole. Talk to him, talk to him.

'Going as fast as I can. Remember, I'm a baker by trade. I'm not used to this sort of work.'

'That's not what I hear,' he said.

'I'm going as fast as I can and I'm raw and tired and I'm sore.'

'You're not the only one. We can't keep everybody waiting.'

'I never learned how to shovel. How can you expect me to do any different?'

At that he seemed to take notice of me in a different way, or perhaps I imagined it. Perhaps the cold had reached my brain. He lowered himself at the knees and spoke evenly and with intense concentration:

'Well, what have you learned?'

What a strange question. But of course typical for a teacher. How utterly predictable. Still, I had achieved the desired result. His attention was off my pace of shovelling. I'd keep it off.

'I know a lot about the evolution and history of baking,' I said.

Clearly interested, the teacher pulled out his silver case and lit number seven. He repeated what I'd just said and offered me one. I shrugged. *Why not?* I took one and he held out a flame until it caught.

I let down the shovel and swung my arms.

He appeared to relax, told me to take a break and tell him what I'd learned about the evolution of baking. I stood by the protected side of the hole and brought to mind all the information I'd gleaned from many books. He didn't hurry me, even though we both heard the truck drive off, minus its passengers.

I picked up pace with the fundamentals; I'd work my way into the story as I picked up the threads, buy ten minutes of rest.

'You should know,' I said, 'the most important rule in baking.'

'And that is?'

'Too much flour and you'll ruin it.'

'I agree,' he said. 'My wife said that once. Nothing worse than floury apple pies. But I'm more interested in this evolution you mentioned.'

Time to remember things, but how to remember things? I called to mind the words from an ancient manuscript, the *Liber Magistri Hugonis Sancti Victoris*, written around 1130 AD. The author gave the reader a memory technique: watch the colour, shape and position of the letters, whether they were the top, middle, or bottom of the page. Pay attention to the letters' surroundings, he said, and you will remember the content better when you need to.

And how right that was. I stood in the hole, on the coldest day I could remember, and I flicked open various books in my mind and put myself by my desk at home, with a small lamp above the book. I turned the pages. And as I remembered my desk, I remembered the pages.

I said, 'Wheat is a great mystery. It shouldn't exist, by rights. Wheat is a kind of accident that happened over a couple of hundred or maybe thousand years. Starts maybe in 8000 BC, in Greece and Iran. The first bread was a hard mix of pounded grains. Tasted horrible, probably. Puking, stomach problems. After a time, people added water because they liked the taste.'

The teacher said, 'So wheat is not a natural crop.'

'That's what you say. I said wheat was a mystery, didn't I?'

He said, 'The chromosome count is different in wheat grains, and scientists can't figure out how it developed.'

'Isn't that what I have said twice already?' I asked.

'You either know that about the count or you don't. It's okay if you don't.'

'That's right.'

'Well then?'

'That's right,' I said.

He shook his head. 'I hope you aren't one of those who knows a bit of everything and most of nothing. A chancer.'

I ignored him and flicked more pages mentally.

'The accident history waited for was baking. Someone got distracted and left a watery bunch of grain on a hot stone near a fire and came back to discover flat baked bread. We know this happened because archaeologists have found burned wheat grains over five thousand years old. The person who returned to the fire probably noticed the smell first, the first smell of baked bread. The smell that brings men to bakery shops at dawn across the globe.

'Like yours.'

I continued before he could take that further. 'Then the next accident. A little afternoon romance in the Stone Age. A bit of trouble with strangers. Whatever made people leave the gruel alone for hours, they noticed later that the yeast had turned the food bad. Hungry, they must have eaten it anyway and liked the taste and the way the bread held together. Leavened bread. The first germ warfare.'

'And where would we be without war?' said the teacher.

'I don't know. We've never been without it,' I said. 'Anyway, they used mixed seeds and barley, and as time passed, people liked the wheat flour better for eating. But the top layer of watery seed made beer.'

The teacher said, 'What little beasts, what magic! The caterpillar makes a butterfly, germs make tasteless grain into food and drink.'

'There's more mystery,' I said. 'Once people could make bread and beer, they stayed in one place. They grew wheat and defended their territory, defended their crop, all because of tiny germs.'

He said, 'The first cities made by germs?'

'Maybe, I don't know,' I said.

'You surprise me. You're more intelligent than I thought,' the teacher said. 'You had us all fooled with the baker routine, didn't you?'

I continued my place in the great story of bread. 'Around the second century BC, professional bakers arrived on the scene. The Roman Empire made people rich, and the rich aren't interested in making bread. The encyclopaedia I read said that the first professional bakers were slaves. I don't feel any shame; I don't mind.'

'And they were happy to do it.'

'And be free? Of course,' I said. 'Then I thought to myself that the history of civilization was the history of bread making. It seemed so simple, so profound. So factual. I couldn't fault it even when I tried, which wasn't often, only at the beginning, since I knew I was right.'

'What happened then?'

'I realized I was on to a great opportunity. People have to eat.'

'No, I mean, what happened as far as bread is concerned?'

'People ate it, I suppose.'

'And the rest is history,' he said, and stood up.

I said, 'History is about bread and war.'

'Surely there's more to it than that.' The teacher walked around the hole. I watched him. 'Anyway, congratulations,' he said. 'Now I know I am dealing with a clever man.'

I threw my cigarette and took up the shovel again. I was

glad of the break, though I needed to move or I'd die right there and then from the cold. As I dug, I realized a great truth: I really had first discovered certainty in baking. Those germs did the same thing every time. You could set a clock by germs.

Now that I was a decent way into the hole and had rested, I proceeded to eliminate the teacher from my mind.

But he wasn't done with me yet.

PROGRESS

Despite what must have been ninety minutes of digging, my head was still above the hole. I was able to watch the townspeople as they waited at the edge of the field.

People look differently depending on the state of their minds. Some in the crowd stared at the sky until they had to rub their necks from the crick; others glanced up and then to each side, then down, obviously more concerned with the ground under their boots; and one or two even brushed the snow off the wall and sat themselves down with a look of complete indifference.

Which was the state of mind I wanted now.

Once, a long time ago, all of two days ago, I was a baker. My life was a routine. I baked, I sold. Then came the third week in November, when the light in the sky grew menacingly from simple stars or the moon to a low yellow burn that grew progressively each night until I heard thunder with it, the boom of cannon. And I knew the war was coming, cap in hand, to visit our town.

I decided that it was not my war.

And I wondered what I would have to do to survive.

WHAT THE BAKER KNOWS

'What else do you know?' The teacher was still at the hole.

I looked up and then across and saw that I was level with his feet. That deep! Progress!

'What does it matter now what I know,' I shouted, 'out in this place?'

'I'm a history teacher,' he said, his voice also raised against the wind. 'I know what I know. My interest is in knowing what you know. Why not humour me for a while? You can work as you talk.'

I glanced over at the soldiers. They still sat in the gun emplacement under a plastic cover. A small fire whipped flames behind them.

The crowd had not moved. All that seemed to change was the weather. We were close to the last hour of light, and however cold it was now wouldn't be anything like the deep freeze after dark. The pine trees bent in the gusts, riddled with snow. I had lost feeling in my feet. I felt wrapped inside a wrapping inside a box. At least I was out of the worst of the wind, down in the hole.

I thought about his offer and guessed that his companionship might make the second half of the work a little easier. So I agreed.

He smiled, took out his silver case and offered me another. We both lit up, and then I took the pickaxe to a layer of stone and roots.

A Quiz

People can look different from hour to hour depending on the angle of daylight. The townspeople, all men or children, most of whom were prosperous or at least comfortable, looked unwell. Some had elbows sticking out of their torn jackets, their ties half decent around a filthy collar. But they wanted to wear them anyway.

Skin can be beautiful if you view it in the right conditions. At sunset I've often noted how red or bronze my skin appears, how it appears to shine as though I were a god or an important figure. These people appeared vacant though, their skin white as paper except for some blue bruises and cuts.

What people do is just as fascinating. I once studied how some men look around them when they are in unfamiliar circumstances, for instance wandering through a strange town, or when they are out to have a good time but aren't quite sure where they might have it. Or when they want to punish someone for a crime not quite established but rumoured to have taken place. That's where the scapegoat originated; at least that's what I've read. All the sins of the town heaped on one goat, which is then ritually exiled.

Hey, goat, here, take my wrongdoing. Now get away from here.

'You are as deep in thought as you are in that hole.' The teacher paced the edge, flapping his arms for warmth.

I called up to him, 'What else is there to do? Do you have any suggestions?'

'I'd rather you talked to me instead of to yourself. We have much to talk about, if you are willing.'

'I'll talk to you, Teacher,' I said, 'if you tell me what you want to talk about.'

He sighed, folded his arms, dropped his chin. 'Let's see what *you* know, Baker.'

'Ah, a quiz for the baker. Go ahead!'

'Any area you'd like to focus on?'

'Pick a battle, a massacre, anything like that. I am a student of human calamity.' I talked smart to keep his interest.

He rubbed his chin and lifted a finger. 'I have something for you.'

'Ask.' I stood ready with the shovel.

'It's more than a simple quiz or a straight answer. I'm thinking of the story behind the story and whether you have a clue about those things.'

'Fine,' I said. 'Pick something vague and then you can say what you want.'

'No, we'll include knowledge of dates in this quiz. I think, though, that we should both take part in this event.'

'What are you talking about? What event?'

He said, 'Wounded Knee.' I felt his gaze.

Wounded Knee. A famous shooting. I ran mentally to my bookcase and looked up the Indian wars. Then I remembered the time my brother came home one afternoon, complaining bitterly that the teacher forced him to take part in a re-enactment of Wounded Knee in class, said the teacher humiliated him. It took me a week to get the story from my brother.

DANCING IN THE SNOW

'If I stop too long, the hole will fill in. This wind makes it very difficult to make any progress.' I heaved a shovel of fresh snow out of the hole and had to wrestle with a gust to keep the shovel in my hands when it caught the flat side like a sail. The snow evaporated.

'I'm sure you'll manage to keep going somehow. Won't be that long anyhow,' he said.

The next shovelful came back in my face. I bent my head and leaned into the storm as it dipped and whipped.

The teacher sighed. 'It's hard to know what really happened out there in South Dakota. So many different stories. They found bodies for two miles, frozen on the snow.'

'What?' I shouted.

He held up two fingers. 'Two miles.'

'Yes, for two days the Indians said a storm was coming,' I said, 'but the weather that morning was a cold clear blue. The ground was white. They said you could hear animals for miles, the seconds tick by. That kind of silence. That's what I've read.'

'Let's set the scene,' the teacher said, facing his palms out. 'It's time the Indians gave up their guns and came in. Dateline: 29 January 1890. The Place: Wounded Knee. A quiet post office, a bridge, a cluster of tents, a hundred or so of Sioux men, about two hundred and thirty Sioux women and children. Deployed around them, five hundred soldiers. The officers chat with the Indians while the search is negotiated. Everyone seems relaxed. The children play.'

He dropped his hands. 'And now, the Baker's account.'

'I only know what you know,' I said. Best to defer to him at this point.

'But Baker, you just said you've read all about it.'

'I heard it from my brother, that's what I meant. He said you made him and the rest of your history class fight the battle using rulers and compasses.'

'Your brother – in my class?' The teacher measured me. 'But yes,' he said, 'of course. Now I see the resemblance. And he had your manner about him.'

He searched the sky. 'The question, though—'

I looked up. 'What question?'

'—was, did he ever learn anything?'

I said, 'Not in your class. You made him an Indian. The Indians lost at Wounded Knee, and my brother came home angry, really angry, I mean, because he got shot early.'

'Because I made him Big Foot, that's why he got shot early.'

'Well, Big Foot or no Big Foot, he kept getting up to fight some more but you made him stay down.'

'Someone had to be the Indians,' he said.

'Not my brother. When he came home, he told us that he wasn't meant to be an Indian or he would have been born one. So we played the battle at Wounded Knee ourselves. We made my sisters the Indians, and we made ourselves the soldiers, and we won.'

The teacher smiled. 'If that's what it takes to get you to talk, then let's do it all again.'

I scratched my head. 'In this hole? In this weather? It's bruising cold, for heaven's sake!'

'It'll warm you up then. Look, you're freezing, I'm not much better, so let's take a break, move around a little, jump up and down.'

I wondered what he was up to. Best to go along with his plans, whatever they were. He was up there and I was down in a hole.

'Okay,' I said. 'But I'll stay here, where I am. The wind stays out of here.'

Then he pointed at me, 'Are you ready?'

And we both looked around us and saw nothing but snow, and we moved like men in combat dodging strikes with ducks and feints.

The teacher spread his hands as if reading something.

'Baker, you just can't beat the news, that's what I say. Nothing like the headline, that's what I say. Well, I'm seeing here – in the *Chicago Daily Tribune* – that THE SIOUX ARE DANCING IN THE SNOW.'

I sang and hopped around in the hole.

'They dance the Ghost Dance, wearing red shirts with stars and crescents and birds on them,' I sang. I knew that wasn't the song they sang, but since I didn't know what the song was, I made it up out of what was true. That way you can get away with a lot in life.

'Hear all about it,' the teacher said, and turned a page. 'And again, the *Chicago Daily Tribune*, MESSIAH EXPECTED TO ARRIVE AT THE PINE RIDGE AGENCY TODAY, WHEN THE SAVAGES WILL FIGHT.'

'They danced for Christ, for Jesus of the Indians to come and end the world,' I sang, 'and give them a brand new one with no white in it.'

And our friends in the *Tribune* say on 25th November: REDS READY FOR A FIGHT.

The teacher turned another page. 'However, in the *Omaha World Herald*, Dec. 1st, the headline goes: INDIANS HAVE NOT AND DO NOT WANT TO FIGHT.

'I wish they'd make up their minds,' I sang. 'The press.'

'The press is a crowd. That's where the word came from. The press of the crowd.'

I sang as my boots scrunched the ice, and my hands groped at the walls for balance: 'The Ghost shirts will protect the red man from the white man's bullets!'

And above me, the teacher dropped his imaginary paper and shouted at the sky: 'And the red man sang, *We will live again. We will live again.*'

My singing voice was well oiled now: 'You can't beat having Jesus fight on your side.'

The teacher circled the hole and his voice dropped. 'Soon six thousand Sioux are dancing the Ghost Dance in the snow.'

I flapped my arms like a trapped gull. The hole was big enough that I could wave a frozen stick. The wind streamed ribbons of snow over us.

'We've got to get their guns,' he said.

I froze, a foot raised.

'What are you talking about? Whose guns?'

'The Indians',' he said. 'Who else's? And sure enough, the soldiers find rifles under the women's skirts.'

'And now Yellow Bird says, *Something bad is going to*

happen. *Something bad is going to happen. Something bad is going
to happen. Something bad—*'

'—is going to happen,' the teacher said, and threw a hand-
ful of snow into the air, where the wind destroyed it. 'That's
how the bullets will bounce off your Ghost Shirts,' he said.

'Is that all Yellow Bird said?' I asked.

The teacher shook his head. 'No. He said one more
thing.'

'What, Teacher?'

'He said what the Sioux always said before going to war.
He said, *Besides, I have lived long enough.*

'The search begins. Twenty Indians approach the soldiers.
They have guns. Many of the soldiers are recruits, barely a
month in the army. Their fingers are wet with sweat and
their hearts are like poppies. They've never been in a fight.
And the Indians have better rifles.'

I said, 'Black Coyote rolls a cigarette and two soldiers try
to grab his Winchester.' I brandished my shovel. 'Wait! The
damn gun goes off.'

'And the Indian wars are over,' the teacher said.

'And the Indian wars are over,' I sang, beating my chest so
that my voice hopped in timing with the blows, the way my
brother did.

He said, 'The twenty Indians threw off their blankets and levelled their twelve-shot Winchesters. A soldier got a bullet
through his nose, it swung loose and bloody on a piece of
skin. People started falling. Ugly, man-to-man. Big Foot falls,
a bullet in his forehead; his daughter falls, dead, on him.'

'I didn't do that!' I shouted.

'The commander orders the four Hotchkiss machine guns
on the ridge to open up on the Indians. It's carnage. Fifty

explosive shells a minute. Canvas pumping fire. Men col-
lapsing with six-inch holes in them. A United States captain
gets the top of his head blown off. Knees shot off. But the
fire from the Hotchkiss guns is murderous. Some Indians
attack with clubs, guns, teeth, knives. To have a chance,
they know they have to stay at close quarters. The soldiers
have a bad commander. He deployed his troops in such a
manner that they fired through the Indians and into each
other. A classic mistake. Maybe they weren't expecting a
fight.'

'Never mind that. Just fire at the tents!' I yell. 'Get them
all into the open!'

'Fire then,' the teacher shouted. 'Don't stop now!'

I held my hands together in front of me like the teacher
had when reading his newspaper, but I was gripping a trig-
ger and reading where the shells exploded: 'And from their
positions on Cemetery Hill, the four Hotchkiss guns, fifty
shells a minute by four, that's two hundred a minute ripping
the whole universe and tearing men and women like wet
toilet paper. The Indians retreat to a ravine, where the guns
can't reach. A few of them, the really good snipers, four of
them, I hear, start popping soldiers. Meanwhile, the women
try to escape. One, in a carriage, draws a gun. A Hotchkiss
responds and she screams. The Hotchkiss keeps firing, at
the tents, at everyone. The officers try to stop the recruits
from indiscriminate shooting, but they're panicking. The
women and children fall everywhere. The Indian men,
enraged at what they see, leave the ravine to counterattack,
and they get cut to pieces.

'A Hotchkiss follows the fleeing women and children.
They get shelled all the way to dead.'

———

The teacher went to his knees, observing me as I sweated in the intense cold, caged in my hole like a fly behind a curtain. 'The Lord God. Forty minutes of gunfire and hand-to-hand fighting. Can you imagine it?' His voice shook, probably from the cold. 'They found some of the women two miles away. They found a child sucking its mother's breast.'

I said, 'They started it. Who started it? They did. With the dancing and the general threats. Threatening everyone with Jesus. The officers liked the Indians, I heard. I've read that no one planned this. A gun went off and the Indian nations died.'

The teacher said, 'Let us not forget Lieutenant Hawkins. The man stood on Cemetery Hill. Snipers were firing expertly from the ravine. A bullet hits a watch in Hawkins's pocket and explodes the parts into his stomach. Time itself got a hold of him with its bare hands. Five operations later they got the last of that watch out of him. A cold, dirty, vicious fight.'

'Enough,' I said. 'What was the score?'

'Twenty-five soldiers, one hundred and fifty Indians, maybe one hundred and seventy. Some died later, I heard. They took a photo of Big Foot the next day, frozen on the snow.'

'Yeah, seen it in a book. He's not moving, very frozen all right. And those numbers sound right.'

'Good. Then what have we learned today?' he asked.

I was irritated. The Grandstanding. Teacherizing. The *We*. I said, 'We have learned the facts.'

He shook his head. 'What facts?'

'What happened,' I said.

'What happened?' he said.

The bastard was echoing me. Trying to get me mad, make a move maybe.

The weather broke in and slapped the teacher's coat, shoved him around, made him grip his own ribs with his arms in pain and shivering.

I said, 'I have something to say here.' I left my shovel beside the pickaxe, and I leaned against the hole wall.

'I'm listening,' he said.

'To be honest, if I had to fight, I'd rather not fight a man who says, *I have lived long enough*. That is a hard man to defeat, a man who doesn't have any days left inside his head.'

He smiled, 'So you are afraid.'

'I'm saying no such thing. It's like the Celts, running naked into battle against the armoured Roman legions. Scared the daylights out of them. A man who says that bullets are just dust, and that life is already over, I don't want to fight a man like that. It's not fear, not easy.'

The teacher sat by the hole. 'I read many myths when I was a young boy. And it's hard to know what's real. I loved reading about the ancient invaders of Ireland who walked ashore out of a swirling mist into a strange land. When I was older I read an explanation: they had burned their boats. They had no way back, no sanctuary, no exit if the fighting went badly. They walked from the smoke of their burning boats and into hostile territory, axes in hand. Imagine that, if you can.'

'Imagine what?' Echo medicine coming right back at him.

He waited a moment. 'Being able to live life like that. Living so that you never look back.'

I said nothing. Kicked the shovel under the wind. But the teacher wasn't finished. 'Maybe you would fear such an enemy, maybe not. You'd hardly know how brave you are until the day. If you get killed, you feel nothing. If you fight and survive, maybe relief.'

'Your point?' I said.

He was lost in thinking. I took the shovel. The wind blew louder now. I spoke to myself, 'Yes, I can imagine living without fear.' (I said that because I liked the way it sounded. I think I read it somewhere.)

And while the teacher drifted in his head, and while the snow filled my eyes, I thought about the ways, and the best days, to die. Cold days, warm days, sunny days, windy days. I couldn't decide. To hell with dying. Dead is dead. Coward or hero. The Indians got themselves chased all over the country. They got themselves worn out. By most military standards of the day, whenever they stood and fought, they did well. They made some mistakes. Waiting for Jesus, now that was a bit of a mistake. But the chief mistake the Indians made was not killing the first, second, fiftieth, and ten thousandth man and every other white man they ever saw, seeing as the white man was the Factory Age and they were the Stone Age. That's what I've read.

The teacher did a rigor mortis of thinking. A bit of a romantic in the teacher. Facts aren't good enough. Has to be a moral too. I once wrote in the margins of a history book: *A romantic is a vulture who writes poems and thinks he isn't a vulture. Always standing around, waiting for something awful to happen so he can write his poems stories essays poems in his kitchen garden living room about this and that awful tragedy in this or that place, wherever, where he will never be.* Something like that is what I wrote.

Down in the hole, the November hole in the November snow field, the world felt bleak to me then. I was alone. Sure, the teacher stood near by, but he stood a galaxy away from me, the baker and his history. And if I believed in portents and sorcery, I'd have been concerned, even worried, at what happened next. You see, in the field, the wind stopped and the sky cleared for something like thirty seconds. We looked, the teacher and I, at the snow falling thinly from the last of the passing heavy cloud. For half a minute the sky was brilliant blue enough to hurt my eyes when I gazed out of the hole. The uncovered afternoon sun slanted against the tops of the trees and lit them with orange. But the next cloud's shadow rolled over the snow, and then the sun, and then over me, like a cold finger. The brief heat did help me feel my skin again, and now the pain was much worse when the dark swept back and the cold wind pushed the world on and on in front of it.

PART II

2:00 p.m.

THE SECOND TRUCK

When I had dug my way below the level of the teacher's feet I made sure to ask him the time.

He made a big show out of consulting his watch, though he did have to hold it close to his face in the low light.

'It's one fifty-six.'

'Just say two o'clock, will you?'

I waited for his follow-up, the smart remark. That didn't come, however, and I took the pickaxe to the next layer of earth and stone. I was about one and a quarter metres down now. That's when the pickaxe struck a band of rock and sent electricity up my bones and nerves so violently that I wanted to vomit. I bent over, but with no breakfast in my stomach, I dry coughed till my eyes teared up.

The shadow filled the edge of my sight.

'Get up.'

'I'm sick.'

'Get up and dig your hole. It's two o'clock. Too late for crying now.'

I was too sick to fight him. I wielded the pickaxe and sparks flew. As luck would have it, the layer at this depth was almost completely rock. The question was, how much more of it? I had to reach two metres by dark, and as I worked I realized that this hole was bigger than you'd think if you were standing at the edge looking into it.

Unfortunately that's what the teacher was doing. I couldn't fight him. Maybe he'd get some sense and know a man can't be pushed beyond a certain point.

As the wind raked sheets of snow off the field, a second truck moved along the lane and stopped just past the gate before reversing back, as the first had done. The driver got out and lowered the rear tailgate. Wrapped in the stretched folds of their clothes, men jumped down and walked uncertainly to the gate and waited. I counted about twenty, maybe thirty. No children this time. A soldier unlatched the gate and pointed to the place in the field where the first group was located. The new group plodded through the snow and joined the others with handshakes and embraces.

The voice from above.

'I said Dig.'

I thought, *Watch it, Teacher. Be very careful.*

I worked in silence for a while, not even acknowledging him when he asked me if I wanted another cigarette or held out his flask of whisky.

I'm sure it was for my benefit, nothing to do with getting the infernal hole done in a reasonable time.

GOOD OLD LEON FIEVEZ

Teachers are used to talking. In a classroom, silence is failure. I could understand why the teacher couldn't leave me alone. Ten minutes passed and he's by the hole again.

'Are we talking?' he asked.

'What about?'

'Sorry about hurrying you just now. Holes can't get finished in the dark. And in two hours the cold is going to be severe. I shouldn't have shouted.'

'We all do what we have to. That's okay.'

I took his offer of a sip of whisky.

'You know, Baker, going back to calamities and massacres for a minute – I suspect we'll never understand why groups of people murder on a mass scale. I wonder—'

'Yes?' I asked.

'If we'll ever be able to measure evil.'

I swung the pickaxe and cracked another few inches of stone.

'I think evil is overrated as a concept,' I said. 'Everything is evil these days. People like you, people who think they're educated and have the right to blow off steam at, you know, students, you make everything a sensation, or sensational, I mean. Blowing everything out of proportion. Stick to the facts, I say. A shot in the grocery store, a man falls, you hardly turn your head. Most killing is very ordinary. You get used to it.'

'And the Baker finally speaks! We have his mind!' He clapped his hands and lit number nine. 'I'll tell you this, Baker, the dead don't get used to it.'

'That's true but irrelevant.'

'Baker, will you get used to it?'

I shovelled the debris clear. Some parts flew back into my face.

'I'm not the real issue here,' I said. 'Historians like you make ordinary events seem like firecrackers were going off and that the whole world stopped. I've got news for you: nothing stopped. People read their newspapers, poured lemonade, rubbed suntan oil, looked at dirty pictures. I don't care what the meaning is of who was killed or what battle took place or who invented what. The ordinary world kept going, the world of people like me. We keep the world going, Teacher. You comment on it. That's how we're different.'

'Never mind.'

'See? You're arrogant.'

'You are right, about evil. Evil is just doing a job.'

'That's not what I meant at all.'

I shrugged my shoulders. No arguing with this man, no changing his mind. I read once that the Buddhists advise that when you are dead set on a course of action you should at that precise moment very carefully consider the opposite course of action. Not this man. He understood too much for his own good. No flexibility. All thought and no reaction.

He said, 'Just doing a job, eh? What about Frankenstein, Genghis Khan, Mr Hitler, King Leopold? An impressive if incomplete list. The better known ones, I suppose, to the uneducated reader.'

The teacher waved his hands in the air as if directing aircraft into a hangar. I think he was trying to stay warm rather than be dramatic, but you never know with these types.

He shouted, 'Let us discuss them all. Let us compare atrocities and mayhem, you and I.'

'Wait a minute. I want to finish what I was saying. I want to say that evil is part of survival, what people like you call evil. Frankenstein made life out of dead human parts to advance science and medicine.'

'He wanted to make his own Adam. Create his own race,' he said.

'So? People have children, don't they?'

'And this artificial creature lived his early life as an innocent, just like children. The world's cruelty made that creature a killer. Even if we got a whole new Garden of Eden, I tell you it'd be the Garden of Evil before long. The Garden of Eden would turn into a toilet in a railway station.'

I said, 'Man is a killer by nature. Everyone wants to survive. What's wrong with accepting that?'

'History is not about survival, and it never was. It's about patterns. We recognize the madmen because they all follow a basic formula of egotism, manipulation, and finally, aggression. The ingredients in every administrator who runs a country or stabs his underlings in the back to maintain his position in a small provincial firm.'

'That's your theory,' I said.

'And yours?'

'My theories come from books.'

'But you mix them all up, you fool.'

My blood rose and I shook my shovel at him.

'You're the fool if you don't understand what survival is! You're doing it now. Both of us are! You don't understand surviving so you call it evil. Dying is good, I suppose. A noble death and all of that. Sorry, not for me. I don't want to know that it's me who dies when history is written. I want to know why me and not someone else, and what I can do to stop it.'

'Don't bother—'

I shouted, 'I'm digging this hole and I want to survive. I believe in survival. I want to live!'

'I can see that,' he said.

'I want to live. I want to!' I shuddered and bent, cursing the ice crawling everywhere on me.

He lit another cigarette. His hand shook. I couldn't tell whether it was the weather or if I'd worried him now, given him pause for thought.

'Medusa,' he said, after a puff that the wind snatched and blasted into nothing.

I consulted my books, the dictionary.

'The bitch with the snake head? What about her?'

'Really, Baker. Show some respect. The mythic creature who turned men to stone if they beheld her.' He spoke with menace, 'Her eyes. The snakes for hair.'

'A good defensive weapon,' I said.

'That's what evil is. That's its face. One look at the face of evil will turn most men to stone. It takes respectable people and makes their blood concrete. They don't even know it's happened to them. The Dominicans launched the Inquisition. They didn't connect the tortured bodies to

Jesus. They connected them to Satan. That's the logic of evil. It's mechanical. It does the job and then makes dinner.'

'Teacher, King Leopold of Belgium. Killed ten million Africans in the 1890s. A business matter.'

'What business?'

'Collecting rubber. I've read that in 1839 Charles Goodyear spilled sulphur in his house and created a substance good for all sorts of industrial use.'

'And where did he get the raw material?'

'It grew on vines in another country.'

'Where were these vines?'

'In the Congo.'

'Indeed, you are right. The Congo.'

And then, on a wild impulse, I counted to three and we said together:

'In the Congo!'

The teacher smiled and twirled on a foot, held his head high and lilted his lines.

'The facts are,' and he acknowledged my interest with a smile and a nod, 'the facts, as my friend the baker is so fond of saying, are that Leopold, strangely forgotten by the atrocity upholsterers, appointed, and let us say that word carefully and with all reverence –'

He gestured to me and we both said, 'Appointed.'

'– some Congo locals, the Force Publique, to a set of responsibilities that included getting villagers to collect sap for rubber. Everyone had a quota. But collecting rubber isn't easy. Know how it's done?'

'No idea. I am a baker.'

'I'll tell you. You had to collect the sap from the vine and spread it across the skin of your arms until it dried, then rip it off, along with body hair or bits of your skin.'

'Nothing you wouldn't get used to. The hair would be gone anyway after the first couple of times.'

'Ah, but waiting until the sap dried on your arms was the problem. You had to stand for days in a flooded forest of vines with your arms spread out until the stuff dried on you, and very few villagers were eager to go through that to collect any sap for Leopold's agents.'

'And Leopold's response?' I asked.

The teacher sat down on the rock and leaned forward as if to explain something to a dull yet promising student.

'The oldest response. The Force Publique took hostages, Baker. On a massive scale. They took something the villagers valued. Took their wives hostage until each man in each village came up with his quota of rubber. Hundreds of thousands of men stood in forests spreading sap on their arms to get their wives back. How slow it must have been, that wait. How agonizing to wait in wet forests for the precious King's dream to dry on your arms until you rip it off, and again, and again, while your wife sat in chains. Rip it off until weeks pass and you have no hair to rip off, no skin, just the pain, the despair of having to stand still for days so you can get someone back. Standing still.'

'Supply and demand,' I said. 'Unfortunate. Little to do with character on the King's part.'

'It really was that simple,' he said. 'Leopold is unique in the phalange of mass killers. It was a business matter, a delegated solution to a supply problem. A solution.'

The teacher stood, raised a finger, and kept talking, this time, I think, to himself.

'Our man didn't harbour any major philosophical differences with the natives; they just happened to live in a
country he owned. No principles kept our good old Leo
awake at night. No racial hatred of any great kind different in
any great way from the average man on the street.'

'But not indifferent. I mean, he had to have known and
thought about it,' I said, 'at night, I mean, when all the
lights were out and he couldn't sleep.' I stopped myself.

'He had a sixteen-year-old mistress. He didn't think about
anything except the sap between her legs.'

'Ha! Funny!' I yelled.

'It is, isn't it? She had a little forest he stood prisoner in.'

'Ha!' I laughed again and then immediately raised another
point to hide my awkwardness:

'Isn't the Congo where they cut the hands off?'

'Yes.'

He looked at his hand, at the wrist, as if it never belonged
to him at all. Something he gouged out of the ground when
the cold sun caught a bit of bone, a hand. The fingers, four
and a thumb, held cups of coffee, book pages, pointed the
way for strangers, stroked hair back, helped words come out.
I saw him looking at this hand he might have found. He
turned the hand in his hand.

Around us, the cloud lay on the field like a fat belly on
white sheets.

He said, 'What happened with the hands. You wouldn't
believe it if you read it in a history book: hands got chopped
off because ammunition was scarce. I'll tell you what happened with the hands. The Belgian agents liked to hunt,
which meant bullets, and bullets were expensive; so they
cut the right hand off living villagers to prove that a man was
dead for each bullet. Bullets were counted: all of them.

Administrators counted bullets and counted hands. They had to match up.'

'And the Belgians rewarded their agents for the hands.'

'Ten million dead,' he said.

'You'd wonder how they got to do it, I mean, that's an awful lot of killing.'

'In a thousand small ways on a thousand different days. With the help of men like good old Leon Fievez.'

'Who?'

'Yes, your test on King Leopold's Congo in 1894 will conclude with the words of one good Belgian army man, Mr Fievez, the humanist.'

I said, 'A philosopher? Never heard of Fievez the philosopher.'

The teacher said, 'A humanist, because when the local villages didn't come up with the goods, he said that one example was always enough:

'One hundred heads cut off, and there have been plenty of supplies around the station ever since. My goal is ultimately humanitarian. I killed one hundred people . . . but allowed five hundred to live.'

An engine revved above the storm. We both turned and watched the truck drive down the lane and into the forest.

The teacher pointed at me.

'Now, Baker, this Belgian officer believed that he was a humanitarian.'

'Sounds so.'

'Very well. And so the question is: was Leon Fievez evil?'

I shook my head. 'Not if he didn't know he was, or wasn't, or thought he was not. I mean . . .' I stumbled on all the little words. I can track them for a while and then my brain gets tired and lets go and I'm talking words.

'What I mean is, he may indeed,' I said, 'have been a good person caught up in a difficult situation. If he knew that what he was doing was not necessary – and we don't have the full picture here – don't know what type of man he was or the pressures he was under.'

'Aha! You contradict yourself, Baker.' He seemed delighted, like finding a favourite fresh pastry under yesterday's goods.

'I contradict nothing of the kind,' I blurted into the driving snow, feeling the flakes pop against my tongue. I wrapped my scarf around my raw throat.

The teacher said, 'I've forgotten the contradiction. It's somewhere in you, though,' and he just stared at me then. 'Make up your mind.'

'My mind is made up.'

'I can't help this!' And he laughed. 'Baker, do you know what fun I'm having?'

'Yes.'

'If you can't judge Fievez's character, then you can't judge anyone in history. Our past becomes an equation that adds up to the present and nothing more. We occupy seats left vacant for us until we vacate them.'

'Precisely,' I said. 'And you do what you must to survive.'

'Chilling,' he said. 'You chill my blood.'

'Yes, I probably do.'

'What's the use of history then?'

I said, 'I learn that it happened. I know how to act. It's like reading a manual to learn how to do something, like build a new oven, not that I've ever needed one.' I paused, 'The art of making bread, you know, never—'

'No, let me . . . never changes!' he said. Another belly laugh.

'It hasn't, not since the biblical era of time.'

His laugh froze like a fork on the air until more replaced it, and more and more. Baker laugh. Bread laugh. Histrionic laugh. Cough laugh. Fist in mouth and tears in eyes laugh. Pull out another shaking cigarette laugh.

Offer one to me laugh.

'No thanks,' I said.

He lit up and I waited for his next move. He enjoyed the power he had over me. I could feel it.

I thought how much I had read about power. What had I learned? That you have it or you don't. And if you don't, you get it or you die without it for ever. You die and you die believing the stuff that says you'll be remembered. And God will say, 'You took nothing. All those other people were there for you. I put them there for you. And you took nothing. You lived the meek life and now you want a reward. I'll give you a reward. Nothing gets nothing.' And he clicks his fingers and I disappear, nobody. And I appear nowhere. Nothing between me and nothing.

Now where did I read about all that? Nowhere, though something like it in German and I had to get a dictionary. *Nichts ist dasein,* or something like that, what the philosopher Hidigger said. *Nichts ist nichtsein nichtig. Gott wrecked* or *recht.*

'God's right hand and left hand,' I said out loud, forgetting that I had been thinking. (I spent so much time alone.) Then I wondered to myself what would happen if God got his hands mixed up on Judgement Day? Does right hand mean his right hand or his right hand from your position in front of him, which would be his left hand? For the love of God, let's not get that mix-up going on the day in question. Upheaval, righteous people head-first into flames. The wicked scratching their heads.

Of course the teacher picked up what I'd said: 'God's hands? With both still attached?' He made a mock search for his right hand.

'I've lost my right hand,' he said. 'Listen everyone, Judgement Day is cancelled, doesn't matter what you did.'

I shouted, 'I am a Christian!' I shouted again, 'And I don't like that kind of talk!'

Seething, I dug, waiting for the teacher to settle down. Had to be careful. He did have a certain kind of power I didn't understand. Came from a good family. Not like me. His mother and father bought bread at my shop. Never said a bad word to me. Never in a hurry, even if she looked at her watch while I moved slowly and sometimes dropped her bread. Spoke lots of languages, spoke softly. His father a professor of economics, no less. Gave speeches when important people came to town. When this present trouble flared up, the professor gave an impassioned speech at the town square. Went off with the soldiers afterwards, people wondering where he went.

I think I know.

I think I know where the teacher's father is.

I have dug other holes.

Things I Know

When I was still a boy a man told me, 'You know a lot of stuff that's never going to do you any good.' But I soon learned this: information is gold. And when I learned how to use information, I couldn't get enough of it. I put it in my pockets, I put it in my brain.

I can recite to you the military tactics of Genghis Khan; the Napoleonic campaigns; machines of war, weapons, supplies; I can tell you how to survive a medieval siege and bake you anything you'd want to eat on a march; and if you insist, debate the philosophy of war and tell you why war is important or why it isn't. I can discuss the technical specifications of the first torpedo, fired in 1777. The bombing missions of World War II. How many died on both sides (estimated, of course) in the Blitz, the Blitzkrieg, the Great War, the Plague, the Hundred Years War. I can analyse cavalry charges, machine-gun technology, why the AK-47 is still the best gun for fast, reliable fire; I know the creep rate of green jelly gas, I know retreat strategies, I know war. I am a student of human battle. Ask me anything. Tell me nothing. I don't care. I've read it all.

OUCH

Maybe he was sorry he laughed at God or at me. Whatever the reason, he took a softer tone.

'Look, surely you don't believe in a Judgement Day?' he said.

I said, 'Of course I do. If there wasn't, we could all do what we wanted.'

Through the white storm, his black eyes watched my every move. The type who misses nothing, this one.

'What about human punishment?'

I said, 'They ought to do more of what they did in the Middle Ages. People only do what they're told if they know they'll pay the price.'

'You'll have to give me an example, something you've read.'

'I believe in more than punishment. I mean penance, saying you're sorry before you die so that you can go to heaven. Make everything a clean slate again.'

'I don't understand one word of what you're saying.'

I had an example ready. 'I read about a Count Fulk who had, well, killed a few people, at least his wife for sure, they knew that, but probably more than that one official kill. And he'd slept around and stole some things. Anyway, this Count felt the end of his life coming and wanted to square things up. And so he went to the local bishop or whoever was in charge and asked what he had to do to wipe the slate clean.'

'Count Fulk. Yes, I've heard of him,' the teacher said.

'People said he fainted when he got the penance. If he wanted to die clean, he had to walk three round-trips to Jerusalem in shackles, across France, Hungary, Serbia, Bulgaria, down through Syria and Jordan into Jerusalem. Three times, round trips. Over twenty thousand kilometres. And whipped on final stretch to the finish line.'

'They whipped a happy Count, no doubt.'

'What else? Imagine, you've got a ticket to heaven. Now that's punishment. Not like the raps on the knuckles you get today. And everyone wins in the end. I'm sorry, bit of pain, the boy goes to heaven.'

'People get off easy today, and that's the truth,' said the teacher.

'Now that's the truth. But if your eyes get plucked out while someone slices off your toes, now that's something to fear.'

We said nothing and I dug a while. Then, with the voice of a man who couldn't swallow a burning question, he said, 'Listen, Baker, you might be able to help me with this.'

'Anything, while I can,' I said.

He asked, 'Should there be a time of reflection, maybe even redemption, before punishment?'

A question I'd never even thought of.

I noted how close he stood to the edge of the hole. This was his big day. The day he got an admission from me, a request for forgiveness; a set of wrung hands, bowed head, a few well-placed tears. I knew he wanted tears from me.

He could wait for tears from me.

'Depends,' I said.

'You know what punishment meant once?'

'Death. My brother says you explained it in class. I read up on it after that.'

'What did you find out?'

'In the 1500s, life expectancy was a lot less than it is now. Half the people died from disease before they got to thirty; for women, twenty-four, on average. They married and died early. Not much time for prison, if that is where all this talk is leading.'

'I wouldn't say that,' he said. 'There was plenty of time for it, but it's just not the way they thought.'

'You're the teacher. All I'm saying is that I read what I just said.'

'They didn't believe in rehabilitation, Baker. That's a fact.'

'So nothing's changed. You made my brother stay in after school.'

'He hadn't learned the lesson for the day.'

He sat on the rock and lit a flame to his cupped hands, watched me.

'My theory on punishment,' he said, blowing smoke, 'is that prison bars have always been invisible: superstition, religion. People went crazy from guilt in those days, Baker. Works its way into your muscles, around your ideas. Black-cloak people the world over, the whole lot of them. If you can make people feel guilty, you have power.'

I smiled because I was angry.

'Speaking of power,' I said, 'Are you powerful right now, Teacher?'

'You're going to get your punishment, Baker, just like your brother. You're going to be kept in very late indeed.'

I glanced at the ground under my boots, now much deeper below the ground under his boots, the frozen rocks battered and prized out with the pickaxe and shovel tip.

I said, 'Threaten me all you want.'

WHAT? MR FIEVEZ AGAIN?

The teacher stood back. I dropped the shovel and went to the side of the hole that faced the gate. The soldiers poured tea or coffee from a billycan. They had tied scarves on their hands and around their necks. Although they didn't make a show of keeping an eye on us, I hadn't a doubt that they could move in a second. Nothing between them and me but fifty metres at most, nothing to block a heavy hail of machine-gun bullets. Behind the soldiers, a desperate crowd doing anything to stay warm. A couple of them had approached the gate soldier and seemed to be asking about gathering firewood or walking around the field. Maybe shelter. He waved them back.

I eyed the teacher. His hand was back in the pocket, making me more nervous than the machine gun because, no matter how less powerful, handguns could be lethally accurate. This hole would soon be deep enough that I'd be trapped in it, unable to jump out cleanly. Scrabbling like an animal while he shot me.

The teacher stubbed his cigarette. I shovelled and kept an eye on his hidden hand. He jumped up and down. 'God, it's cold.'

'It is that,' I said. 'It's cold and we're not finished yet.'

'We shouldn't let a discussion about the weather intervene at this point,' he said.

'No, Teacher.'

'Now, where were we regarding the good Mr Fievez, late of the Belgian army?'

'Whether he was evil,' I said.

'And your answer?'

'None. What's relevant is what I learned from reading about him. Strategy. Survival. What does it matter if I think him good or bad? Will Mr Fievez's victims live again because I take sides all these years later? Come teacher, answer me this—'

I raised my hands to him in a plea of sorts.

'Yes?' he said.

'What's the point in history, yourself? What good does your long telescope into the past do for you? You think I'm stupid. I know you do. But I'm not stupid. Believe me.'

He laughed. 'I doubt very much that you are stupid. I think you are the cleverest man I've ever known.'

He pointed to his watch. 'It's twelve minutes past two.'

I didn't see him actually look at his watch. That made it a guess.

A Skirmish in the Bakery: The Art of War

If you are far from any danger at all, study strategy. When things are going well, get ready for the rough stuff by reading strategy. When things get rough, apply strategy.

I've read a lot about strategy.

If you want to stay out of trouble, make your calculations beforehand. That's what the general says. What general, you ask. Very well, I'll answer that even though I don't have to say anything if I don't want to. Sun Tzu's *The Art of War*, a manual written by a Chinese general 2,400 years ago, is the only literature I've ever learned by heart. At least I've memorized bits of it, that's what I mean. The oldest war manual in the world, written for those who want to win, it reveals the age-old sciences of manoeuvring, strategy, attack, all those things.

After I discovered the book in the library (now a billet for the green-uniformed troops), I saw how I could use it for anything to do with people. Look, when you run a bakery in a medium-sized town you do battle every day with citizens from ravenous and poor to filthy rich and over-nourished. It's a battle. I carried the manual with me to work for the first couple of months after I opened under my proprietorship. I had a few problem customers.

———

I applied the science of manoeuvring to the policeman's wife, a woman with two suspicious hands and a pair of eyes that bulged over my food, her brain eating what she didn't buy. Mrs Policeman, I called her. She thought she had the right to frisk all the loaves for freshness and decide, after pawing everything, which one, I repeat one, loaf to bring home. I never made much money out of her and resolved to stop her contaminating the bread. And besides, other customers watched her, and I guessed they wanted to see how I was different from the old baker.

One day she marches in with a sigh that's supposed to be a greeting. Attitude now.

I walked to the counter, the whiff of fresh loaves in the air, rubbing my hands in my apron. As usual, I talked without meeting her gaze.

'And what can I get you today?' Being even mildly polite cracked my face.

A sideways glance at me, out comes her hand, stroking the apple-walnut loaf, a pricey item and not something people will buy with finger marks or red nail polish all over it. She digs her index finger in, mumbling *Fresh* or something like that.

I inhaled sharply and said, 'Yes, very fresh. No need to test. Today's bread, made at dawn. Yes, fresh, tasty bread. You want it?'

Hmmmm. *Of course no answer.* How about this one? A finger trailed, fingernail nibbled at a carrot-flavoured flatbread. I'll be damned if she wasn't about to taste it without buying. I buzzed around her, keeping busy but always close to her, wiping things that didn't need wiping, counting items already checked. No, she didn't get the hint.

After another couple of days of this I carried to work a complete paperback translation from the Chinese of *The Art of War* and placed it behind the counter, ready for her next visit. I propped General Sun's manual open at the section 'Army Manoeuvres', with a slice of pumpkin pie holding the pages flat in the middle. I had underlined one instruction from the general in the certain knowledge that I'd need it: *Disciplined and calm, wait for disorder and the enemy's clamour: this is the science of retaining self-possession.*

I dusted, paced lightly, walking on the balls of my feet. Checked things I knew were done. A couple of customers, an uneasy silence, people in slow motion as before a great battle. I did not have long to wait. The town bell struck eight times and the sun broke through the tops of the houses, and her shadow passed the window, and the handle on the door turned. Her handbag, yes, definitely hers, a right shoe, golden nauseating yellow, and the fur, of course the fur, and last, partially covered by a blue head scarf, her moon face. The entrance itself a work of art, so silent, her instincts as sure as those of the assassin on hashish, the spy at a political meeting. Knows where to look, whom to avoid. Clicks as she closes the shop door, three steps to the counter. Eyes on the breads, the expensive ones. But I had placed them in a defensive position under a glass case, reachable only by tongs from my side. As Sun wrote in 'Strategies of Attack': *The best warfare strategy is to attack the enemy's plans.*

I attacked her plans with glass, walls of glass.

Remembering my yoga, I breathed deeply into my stomach and smiled.

'Good morning.'

Perplexed at the change, she removed a glove and moved her finger, pressed it against that invisible strength. She might have thought it was an illusion. *Maybe he won't notice that I'm doing this even though he's standing right in front of me and no one else is in the shop except me and him.*

I stiffened, every muscle poised for movement. Breathe deeply. Breathe deeply. I lowered my eyes to the manual, where I'd underlined a different instruction under 'Manoeuvres,' partly obscured by some crumbs: *Avoid attacking an army that is confident and well formed: this is the art of studying circumstances.*

I resisted the urge to move to defend the cakes and marvelled at my restraint, even when she reached out and touched the glass covering and deftly slipped her hands across the top and under it, located the rim, and applied firm pressure to move the top away and expose the products. I gasped. I needed no book now. General Sun's voice roared in my ears: *As rapid as the wind, as tight as a forest. Let your plans be elusive and dark as night, and when you strike, fall like a thunderbolt.*

From her point of view I must have moved at light speed and my elbows must have materialized from thin air, so quickly did I lean my elbows on the glass. I cradled my face in my hands and in a bored tone said, 'What can I get you this morning?'

She knew she was outmanoeuvred.

'I'd like . . .' glancing over to the door, 'I'd like . . .'

'Yes?'

'Some bread.'

I moved one elbow and swept a hand over the counter in a generous arc, 'Oh, I have bread.'

'I want that bread.' She pointed at the far end of the counter, where all the cheap ryes and flatbreads were wrapped in plastic, stacked, no covering, clearly marked and priced because that's what poor people value most.

A cheap attempt at getting me to leave my position unguarded for easy access to the jewels.

'Just select what you want,' I said.

Her voice testy. 'I need your help.'

I said, 'Point out something and I'll be glad to assist you. I have to check some prices, you see.' I lowered my eyes to the manual as she walked to the cheap bread section and sighed heavily. Not a woman used to being outflanked. Then she left.

Next day she was back as if it was her first time in the shop, all smiles and greetings. Different perfume.

'Good morning,' I said.

'And a very good morning to you,' she said. Jaunty step. Approached the glass behind which I had placed myself, *The Art of War* laid flat on the open cash till, with the chapter 'Planning Attacks' in clear view, and a single line I'd marked with an asterisk: *All warfare is based on deception.*

Deception is the middle name of all women, I knew that, of course, but isn't that another matter altogether, and I knew that she, the lady of the manor, even if a policeman's manor, would employ a tactical type of surprise. I imagined that the preceding night she stayed awake into the early hours drawing up her plan of attack to get those cakes and feel them. Studied the ground of battle carefully. Made notes while her husband slept and the television snored. Woke from a short hour's sleep, dressed for battle, swallowed a cup, out the front door, off to the Battle at Baker's Shop.

'And what can I get you this morning?' I asked.

She was not the only one who had studied all night for today's struggle.

After work, I had gone home, ate frugally, then took the Sun manual from its hiding place in the bread basket and read through a bottle of good wine and then under my covers with a torch in case anyone suspected I was studying anything. I concluded that if she were smart she'd follow the Chinese master's advice on where to attack: *The spot where we intend to fight must not be made obvious; for then the enemy will have to prepare against possible attacks at different points.*

Using a pencil (easily erased evidence) I had mapped her possible strategy.

Her best option: she'd catch me unawares if she simply went straight for the cheap rye breads at the far side of the counter from the expensive stuff; by the time I gathered myself to confront her she'd have pounced on the glass top and lifted it.

Fingered the fruit breads.

Sitting on my bed under the bulb, I thumbed voraciously through the Chinese war book. Yes, I had much to think about. Learn, memorize, repeat aloud. I felt no hunger, you see, no thirst. I just felt the heat of battle, the thrust of steel into a soft belly. And then, propped up by a pillow, I covered 'The Nine Situations.'

And at once I had the key to victory. With the terrain of the shop fixed firmly in my mind, I mapped a strategy.

Then it was dawn and time to leave for the bakery. I moved cautiously, my briefcase with the plans tight by my side.

After the morning's baking I opened the briefcase and put the plans into motion by piling some pastry boxes near the window like a pillbox in Normandy and lay beside them on the floor. I took a white cap from my pocket to blend me in with the white tile. One careful set of fingers slid the binoculars from the briefcase and a pair of sharp eyes scanned the street for signs of activity. Good. Nothing yet. I taped a sheet of paper to the floor just to the right of my head for easy access in the heat of battle. On it, the general's instructions for observing and interpreting enemy movements. His first advice: how to detect an unseen enemy. *If trees move in the forest, he advances.*

I focused the binoculars. The blur of distance turned into the newsagent's, a little bit down and across the street. I observed the agent as he untied the string from the packs of newspapers, lit a cigarette, and stuck his finger up his nose.

I swung the opticals to the left and right, nothing but the sun catching the street and fencing the night into a retreat. If the policeman's wife was around, she was good, damn good. The lens felt like two hot rings. I briefly checked my Swiss Army watch: 07:09. I wanted to see her coming. The general's next lines: *If the birds rise, he lies in ambush.*

So birds sit on branches and see reflected metal or movement from soldiers in the undergrowth and fly off in fright. I'm sure at this point, if he sees the birds take fright, the enemy is muttering *Bastard birds,* but it's too late to curse the birds, my friends. You should hope that I'm a coward and that I'll let things be until night falls and we can both slip away.

Something moved on the pavement across the street. I grabbed the binoculars and then realized I didn't need them. The milkman left a bottle on someone's windowsill and the curtain stirred and he waved at the person inside. Curtains shifting, a certain sign of the enemy observing you: *If dust reaches high in columns, his chariots advance.*

Yes, the milkman's van; another man with a schedule to keep. I tracked him, then swung to the other end of the street in case the policeman's wife slipped across the road while I was distracted: *If dust is low and spread wide, his infantry is advancing.*

I observed the town doctor stroll into the chilly morning. I magnified him. His right hand shook. Noticed that first about a year previously when I had to get some pills from him. Wouldn't want that hand snipping at my vital parts. Smelled drink off him too, I did, in his office in broad daylight.

I muttered, *Good morning, Mr Doctor.* Why are you looking around you like that? Spent a little time with the mistress, eh? The one who is not presently your wife and who has a nice little place in the town square? Go on, yes, into your car. Close the door, rub your hands, keep the head down. Ignition. Off with you. Out of focus. Gone. *If dust is scattered, his men gather firewood.*

'Hello!'

A shrill voice behind me. 'Could I have one of these?'

'Jesus,' I said.

The boy stood behind me with a loaf and a coin.

'How the hell did you get in?' I asked.

He looked at the door and then at me, the binoculars, the pill box, the white hat.

'I walked in the door. I wondered what was wrong. I've been here for a couple of minutes.'

'Okay, that's okay. Just leave the money on the counter.'

'I want my change.'

'I'll give you the change later.'

He hesitated, so I turned, 'Get out and come back later or leave the money on the counter and come back for the change.'

He said, 'At one o'clock I'll be out of school and then I'll come back,' he pointed to his watch, 'because then I need it for my lunch.'

'Why?' I asked.

'Why what?'

'Why are we still talking? Will you get out?'

He backed out, facing me. 'My mother says that you are a strange man and that you were always very strange.'

'Take the bread and go.'

Shortly after eleven o'clock, Mrs Policeman arrived at my shop door and read a hand-painted sign, BACK AT TWO. I was stooped behind the counter at eye-level, watching her. At first she ignored it, tried to push in the door, realized it was indeed locked, then fingered the sign like she did my bread, as if testing its age. Maybe it was an old sign. A compulsive tester, this woman. *Go ahead, doubting Thomas,* I thought. Touch that sign and see if it's real!

I waited until she had walked away a little bit, frustrated and angry, then I ran to the shop door and opened it with a loud 'Good morning!'

She looked at me in surprise as I stood at the door and gestured her in with the confidence born of a man who for hours previously had read Sun's precise directions on how to prepare for battle on nine types of ground. She stepped forward and back, clutching her handbag, and brushed past me into the shop.

'Bitch.'

'What?' she said 'What did you say?'

I said, 'Which types of bread can I get you this morning?'
'Oh,' she said, and glanced at the counter. Gasped.

Sun's nine types of ground are specific because the good
general fought in all of them and no doubt lost more than a
few men as he learned the correct formulation for his battle
tactics: *There is uncommitted ground, marginal ground, contentious
ground, open ground, intersecting ground, critical ground, difficult
ground, surrounded ground, and fatal ground.*

As I studied Sun I looked up the words in the dictionary
and the commentary given by the translator.

*When the rulers do battle on their own ground, this is called
uncommitted ground.* Some ancient commentator had written,
'The general means that the soldiers are near to their homes
and could scatter at any moment.' That made sense. If things
got bad I could do a runner back to the house, get my few
things, and be off to another town within the hour. I'm a
portable man!

*When one enters the other's ground but not deep, this is called
marginal ground.* The commentator wrote, 'The Chinese
believed that at this point you should burn all boats and
bridges so that the soldiers understand they cannot go back.'

Mrs Policeman walked into the shop till she reached my
marginal ground.

She asked, 'What have you done with the baker's shop?'
'It's my shop now.'

I had made some changes. A chair in a strategic place, on
top of the glass counter. Some postcards placed on it, and
cardboard boxes forming a defensive wall. Nothing an innocent person would notice.

She muttered. I thought I heard her say, *For now.*
'What?' I asked.

'For how long will you be keeping this layout?' She smiled her way back to polite.

'For as long as I need it to keep my produce looking its best. Now, what can I get you?'

I flanked her on the right, moved to the counter and slipped behind it, keeping one eye on her hands. *Smooth and perfect, no work for years*, I'd have said. A kept woman. *They are the dangerous ones.* Although at one moment gripping her bag, those hands could be on my cakes in a blink: *Where it is advantageous if you occupy it and dangerous if the enemy occupies it, this is called contentious ground.*

The contentious ground was the glass case covering my baby delicacies, my fruit cakes. Of course she made straight for it, even though she saw that I had placed a chair on top of the case on which I had built a house of local postcards and some from places I'd never heard of: 'Choice Views of the Countryside,' 'A Village Church,' 'Sunset in the Fields.' If she so much as tilted the glass, the chair would crash down. Any attempt to move the chair would send the post-cards sliding and cracking when they hit the glass. No secret pawing now. That's my postcard alarm.

Where each side can come and go is called open ground.

Mrs Policeman paced the shop. I followed her like I would a slow tennis ball in a one-man match. Looking at my watch. She was a deer stuck in the headlights. Just when I expected her to bow out gracefully, a young girl swung open the door and proceeded to the counter with a large list and her purse. Mrs Policeman looked up, assessed the situation, and smiled.

Where ground forms the key to three states, and the first one to reach it has most of the empire at his command, this is called intersecting ground. The girl was here because I had a stand-ing order with the factory she worked at, an account I inherited with the shop. She came over at the same time every day for bread for the entire shift of twelve's morning break. An important account.

I hurried to the back to pick it up. When I returned, the woman had positioned herself beside the girl and had placed her hands on the chair, her eyes on the cakes. The policeman's wife wanted to make her move in the comfort of company. Maybe she thought I wouldn't do anything if there were wit-nesses. As Sun said, *On intersecting ground, form alliances.*

I came around the counter and handed the girl the large stuffed plastic bag.

'Here's your order. Ten per cent off today because I was closed for a few minutes. I hope you weren't waiting.'

'No,' said the girl. I rang up the discount even as the woman's smile crinkled under her scented-powder make-up. The girl beamed at me, counting the change and the ciga-rettes she'd get for the change at the newsagent's down the street. As she left the shop I made myself busy with dusting what turned out to be mostly air because the counter was clean; I needed to move my hand around a bit.

Mrs Policeman drew in a breath and I could tell she was plotting to kill me or make some kind of a charge. I know that once you cross the threshold of violence, you can't retrace your steps without combat (I think I got that in *The Art of War*, no that's me, I think): *Where an army enters deep into enemy ground, with many fortified cities to its rear, this is called critical ground. On critical ground, plunder.*

Her wig. I had to get her wig. I kicked and gouged my way through the cardboard boxes and flour sacks I'd piled as a defensive wall: *Mountain forests, marshes, ravines, and wetlands, country hard to cover; this is called difficult ground. On difficult ground, press on.*

'I'll take two of these,' she said.

She pointed down at the rye breads with a trembling finger. I glanced up from heaving a flour sack to one side. Nothing but a feint designed to throw me off, make me go the other way. Battle tactics. Very nice. Then she pulled at her hair, a strand of it, and she stepped towards me before I had cleared my way through my own defences.

Two sacks and a few broken boxes to go. One eye on her and two on the job and one on the fruit cakes, three hands grabbing the flour sacks and seven hands flinging the cardboard out of the way. *The exit made on tortuous paths where the enemy can attack with few men, this is called enclosed ground. On enclosed ground, be prepared.*

I was stuck like an octopus heaving stuff to the left and right.

The ground on which fighting with full force will save an army from destruction, and not doing so will cause it to perish, is called fatal ground. On fatal ground, do battle. She took her chance. All her battalions at once with lightning force. She attacked not me but the chair, going after what I valued most; she grabbed a leg and flung it, and the postcards fluttered like snow until they came down and one caught me in the eye and paper-cut me on the lip, somehow on the lip. But of course.

'God, that hurts,' I roared.

I broke free of the last obstacle and flung myself at her with a loaf of bread. She stepped aside, and my fingers clutched at her hair: I grabbed her wig and I pressed against her with the loaf until she was against the wall. I humped her a little. She stood with her mouth open and shut at once, bald-headed with a red bump on her crown. She felt it with tentative fingers, her eyes horror. And I looked at the wig and knew that I had grabbed in my moment of defeat the thing any woman values the most. Her vanity. She pushed me and ran for the door.

'Wait, madam, you forgot this. Not the rye, this!'

She clung to her coat. It dragged after her. She lost one of her heels.

I rushed to the case and took three fruit cakes and followed her along the street and flung them at her fur coat like mortars. All missed, exploded in my hands really, squirted from the pastry layers, trickled down my arms and even under my right armpit.

And I yelled words that came out all chopped up and spitty:

'Try this! Taste this!'

The woman stopped and leaned to the wall. No more of that finger-on-the-cakes nonsense. Look and buy. Look and buy. Don't touch my food!

Thank you, General Sun.

I picked her wig from the cardboard mess and hung it from a brush handle.

I checked the street with naked eyes and then with the binoculars. The enemy had left the field. Run off. Most likely to her husband, an official man with certain official friends. Let her. I'll be here, baking and serving every day from the crack of dawn. I have friends too. Two thousand years of strategy. A Chinese general behind my counter, or in my pocket if I'm at home. If her husband comes in here to berate me, he'd better be careful, that's all. Hubby better be careful.

———

How long did I have to wait for hubby to turn up? Less than an hour. That's how long it took for a figure to appear in his long, flowing black coat in the open door, pointing the longer arm of the law at me (one of his arms was gone at the hand, some sort of war injury from years back, I had heard).

'I've had a disturbing report,' he says. He asked me to explain to him what had happened. As though a member of the public and not his wife had told him about it.

'She tampered with my food,' I say. The cop listened but he didn't believe me. Said his wife said that she kept asking for things and that I wouldn't answer her. She told him that I 'was staring out into space.' She said she'd asked for the rye bread because that was the easiest thing to buy and that I got this 'look of rage on my face and attacked her.' And again, with cakes, after she escaped 'with her life,' the policeman said gravely.

'Rubbish,' I said. I invited him to prove it. Her word against mine.

He left with threats, etc.

After he was gone I saw the wig on the brush handle in full view. The man hadn't seen it. Must have lost an eye in the same war.

But the bakery shop skirmish with his wife is not what got me into trouble.

Running Late

Evening comes quickly on a winter's day. And sometimes the light flows out of the sky as if someone has left a sink plug slightly open. Drip, drip, drip, going, *gone*. Getting to the time when the amount of dark in the air balanced with the amount of light. The storm grew. The wind blew constant and the snow drove horizontal to the ground. My head protected by the hole. I had been digging hard, almost one and a half metres down, the last bit mostly stone.

The teacher strode out of the dusk and held his watch arm to his face.

'It is now 2:20 p.m. on November 25th,' he said. 'You are running late.'

He stood over me with his watch. I owned my own business, looked after it, protected it; this kind of supervision was not supposed to happen to me any more.

Shouts from the field. The crowd. I heard someone say, 'Information. We want information.'

Where to Find God in a Snowstorm

'Do you think that someone listens to people in trouble?' the teacher said. 'I mean, do you think that any god listens to them all?'

I pretended to think and said, 'I doubt that very much. Heaven and earth are big places, never mind all that space out there.' I spoke without stopping my work, a little worried about why they had left me so long out here.

'Or maybe God is deaf,' he said.

I said, 'As a Christian, that offends me.'

He lit another cigarette, smiled down at me.

'Why, I never said anything about a Christian anything.'

'I'm a Christian, so I took it that way, what else do you expect?'

'Of course you did. I could respond, as the philosopher said, that the first and last Christian died on the cross. What I mean by "deaf" is the absurd hope that a supernatural being will intervene, stop what humans do to each other. I don't have that hope any more. God isn't at home or isn't listening. How can you come to any other conclusion?'

I threw down my shovel. He straightened then, expecting an attack, perhaps. The day jerked on its side as I rose to full height.

'I am a Christian, and what you said is offensive to me.'

The teacher ignored me and gestured at the sky, standing with a fist raised like some revolutionary leader calling on the masses in the public square:

'Come on, God, wave a wand. We need magic to save us today. You don't have to prove a thing. You don't have to appear. I will respect your privacy.'

Then the teacher shivered. 'God's a ghost. Baker, listen to me now.' And he shook a finger at me. 'He's behind every closet. And we put him there. Ointment for our oldest fear: that we won't survive. So we take God out occasionally as needed. *I'm tired, let's have some God. My mother died, my father, give me some God. I'm sick and I can't get well: where did you leave the God last time you used it? Is there any God left in the bread basket? Don't tell me we've run out of God, I told you to get some!'*

I shook my head and spit flew out of my mouth. 'That's pure blasphemy! That's outrageous! You will pay for that!'

His voice dropped then, or the wind blew harder, I'm not sure. He spoke in my direction, then away, towards nothing in particular. To an onlooker, a strange and unsettling apparition: a man, this man, moving his lips in a snowstorm, talking up to God in a snowstorm, talking to the sky, then to the ground, conversing with a deepening hole in the ground.

With nothing else to do, I noticed that he had dropped into a reverie, and I commenced digging again, heaping shovelfuls over the side, which would have further perplexed anyone watching. This man stands between heaven and earth, his whole life squeezed between the sky and the ground.

Such is the life of men, I have read.

The teacher cupped a hand to his ear and cocked his head upward. He widened his eyes and turned to me with a short, bitter laugh.

'See – no answer from God to a simple, direct question!'

I crossed myself and looked up at the sky.

'God exists,' I said, staring at him from the hole.

'Ha!' he shouted. 'Well if he did indeed exist, why would he allow something like you to exist?'

'I exist, and that's all you need to know, you bastard!'

He knelt at the edge of the hole and made an exaggerated motion of whispering a secret: 'You know, they talked to God in the city, but the Devil answered.'

'You'd know all about that,' I said, and swung, cracking open pockets of stone layer.

After I'd hacked a few minutes I looked up and saw that he had calmed down, was back sitting on his rock throne. Maybe his delirium originated in the hypothermia he must have been experiencing, despite the long coat. He wasn't moving around much, after all. He could have been one of the crowd over by the wall. The snow was building on his shoulders. I was far enough into the hole to see him only from the knees up.

I shouted, 'I don't know where this bitterness comes from, Teacher. When did you lose your faith in heaven?'

His lips moved. 'Never had it, don't think so.'

'Will we hold court on the existence of God now?' I said.

He sat there, like a man who had taken a drug.

'What do you think, Teacher, that's what I want to know!'

The wind, unmerciful, rattled the barn fence. The temperature went down, it seemed, by the second now. I was glad that the hole protected me. Still, I shielded my eyes and tried to keep the teacher in view.

He spoke with his hands cupped around his mouth.

'Christians.'

'What of them?' I yelled. 'What now?'

He stood up with his hands cupped.

'If you gave them heaven, the honey and milk and mansions, they'd be fine for a while until some of them would –' he knelt and placed his elbows at the edge of the hole so that our faces were close '– develop a better definition of how to live in heaven. How to eat honey, what temperature, what infinity means now that they're in it and, well, bored. Meetings, arguments, leaders. A schism, a minor version of angels falling to earth, or an awkward silence in the halls of bliss, something like that. In theory, they don't trust humanity, don't trust anyone. If I could, I'd write a scene in heaven where thousands of millions of them sit around and listen to sermons from each other.'

'Thank you for the speech!'

I saw him smile through his blue cheeks.

I said, 'I hardly understand a word you've just said. You like doing that to me, don't you?'

He shook his head.

I said, 'It makes you feel superior to me.'

'It doesn't.'

'It does.' I split a stone with the pickaxe.

'It doesn't. Let me do this. Let me tell you that— No, maybe later.'

'We don't have time for laters.'

'Should we light a fire?'

'No, let's get this done,' I said. 'Besides, a fire wouldn't warm me in here.'

And I worked for another ten minutes until I had to wrap my hands under my arms and jump around in the hole to generate some warmth. The teacher looked at me as he lit up.

'Do you really believe all that stuff about angels, land of honey, Garden of Eden?' he asked. 'In a place like this, today, with all this going on?'

I said, 'I wonder about heaven, and of course I believe in it too.'

'Why?'

'I can't say,' I said, 'not the way you can.'

'Use your own words.'

'How about a fairy tale?' I said.

The teacher smiled. His features relaxed, and he genuinely seemed to warm to me for the first time.

'A fairy tale,' he said, closing his eyes as if to savour a delicious chocolate. 'It's been so long. So long. Yes, please.'

He moved over on the rock and tapped the free part, 'Yes, come on, sit down.'

At about 2:40 p.m. on that blustery November afternoon, I climbed out of the hole and sat beside the teacher.

The Fairy Tale

We huddled and I took a cigarette from him as well as a good draught of the whisky. Across the field, the figures in the crowd melded into the landscape, part of the trees and the snow and the wall.

I swallowed and said, 'I believe in heaven because I want to. But I can also prove that it has to exist.'

The teacher's breath smelled of drink and smoke. 'Then you'll do better than any philosopher has. But I really wanted a fairy tale. Don't disappoint me, Baker.'

'I won't disappoint you with how I reached certainty on this matter. Here's what I will do, Teacher. I'll speak as if I were you. I'll say what I think you'd say. I promise, you'll be impressed with what I've learned about you.'

He said, 'Then I really must hear your story.'

And with his big herringbone coat thrown over part of my lap, I traced out my first words with a big stick in the snow.

'Once upon a time Mathilde and Torson died and went to heaven. Their journey to heaven is unimportant.'

The teacher said, 'If this is a fairy tale, a child would want to know everything. They believe, so they need all the details.'

'Okay,' I said, because I wanted to show the teacher that I understood what children needed to know. I said, 'The details need to be right for children. Adults skip words, but for children, words still have power.'

'I agree,' said the teacher.

'Mathilde and Torson closed their eyes—'

'Daddy, how did they die?' It was the teacher who addressed me as *Daddy*, playing the curious child.

I played along.

'Well, child, they died in a traffic accident on a lonely winter mountain highway, so they could not get any help in time,' I said, closing off any further questions about hospitals and doctors and treatment. 'And they opened their eyes in a valley, a green valley with lots of yellow flowers—'

'What type of flowers were they, Daddy?'

'Daffodils.'

'So it must have been spring in heaven, Daddy?'

'It was indeed spring in heaven, and what a beautiful season! The yellows of the flowers set in the lush grass, mowed in places, wild in others, with lots of trees—'

'Daddy, what type of trees?'

I struggled to stay in character. He was pushing it. 'Too many trees to list individually, but some fragrant, some trailing their leaves in the slowly flowing river over which birds swooped and sang.'

'Did the birds catch anything, like fish or insects, and eat them?'

'No killing in heaven, child.'

'So how do the birds live?'

'That's a big secret, I think. I haven't been told anything about that.'

'Okay, Daddy.'

'And remember, this is the tale I have learned. I cannot add anything to it.'

'Yes, I believe you,' said the teacher. 'I'm interested now too, as well as the child.'

I continued, 'And the clothes they wore were soft white cotton, scented with a perfume they couldn't recognize. And the birds sang, but Torson and Mathilde couldn't recognize the sounds; they knew it must be singing, even though the notes were not notes and the sounds not birdsong. And another thing, the light was different. With it they saw the shapes and shadows as in their previous life on earth, yet the light was of a different hue and quality. They could touch it, like a soft furry toy, and shape it, like a piece of putty, and move it around and leave it places where the dark was. But they decided not to play with the light. Maybe they'd drop it and break it and be in eternal darkness. And then they realized that they had decided this without even speaking to each other.'

'Magic,' said the child.

'Then Mathilde and Torson spoke to each other without speaking and decided to speak to each other using words. But when they tried to speak, strange singing noises came out of their mouths on little wings that fluttered around in the soft, furry light. They laughed and even more little wings, attached to tiny bodies, flew out in circles, criss-crossing. It was fun to interrupt each other and see the lines of flight twisting into each other. After a minute, the wings disappeared, so they learned to speak in short sentences and observe the patterns for connections between certain words.

'They thought that maybe this was heavenly writing, but not with a pen or anything like that,' I said.

'Magic.'

I continued, 'Mathilde and Torson decided to wander a little before the sun went down, though when they looked up into the sky there wasn't a sun, but instead a very pleasant feeling of the light brushing against their skin.'

'Yes, Daddy, like through my bedroom window at night when it's warm.'

'Exactly. So they walked across the valley floor and up a gentle slope, and you'll never guess what they saw.'

'What, Daddy. What? I mean, what, Baker, what did the two dead people see?' asked the teacher, which I felt was a deliberate attempt to strangle the special atmosphere of fantasy and suspense I'd managed to weave. But I ignored him and answered the imaginary child instead.

'What they saw amazed them so much that Torson had to sit down. Mathilde clapped her hands in delight.'

I followed the teacher's eyes. I heard a truck and saw a pair of headlights scour the trees.

I resumed the tale:

'What did Mathilde and Torson see? Well, stretched out below them was lush valley grass and people dressed in white. Mathilde and Torson felt happy now that they had company and went down the hill, waving and singing all those wings. The people ran to greet the new arrivals.

'Mathilde said, "They're shouting something. Look, lots of wings. Hang on, they're saying, 'Have you seen him? What do you know?'"

'"Mathilde, I must say you've learned all of this quite quickly," shouted Torson. He saw then that the wings registered shouts by increasing tenfold. He decided never to shout again because it obscured what he was saying, which is what usually happened in real life too.

'"Torson, what do those people mean?" Mathilde said.

'"I have no idea," said Torson, who spoke slowly so that his wings would space well and be legible.

'The crowd read the air over Mathilde's and Torson's heads and looked disappointed. One of them pushed his way to the front and spoke skyfuls of wings. Mathilde couldn't read anything. Torson, who himself had been impatient in life, recognized the patterns. He read slowly from the scribbled chaos above the man's forehead, which he translated as:

'"What do you mean you haven't seen him? Where have you come from?"'

The teacher said, 'What happened then, Daddy?'

'When Torson and Mathilde couldn't answer, the crowd walked back to the valley. What they searched for was a big mystery, though. From all the wing loops that trailed in the air, Torson and Mathilde deciphered a few things: they had found some dung, and it might be the dung that would talk. An important person suggested they move it on a shovel into the open, but one of the women retorted that if anything divine were indeed in the dung, a shovel would be a hugely disrespectful way to transport it. So they carefully and respectfully placed their ears to the dung.

'As they did this, one of them said, "We await your word."

'At length they concluded that nothing lived in the substance, as one of them now called it, because it would have said something. The dung revealed nothing, no matter how they prostrated themselves. "Might be caked, looks a little old," one of them said. "If I can just break it a little," and he lifted it. The women shrieked as it fell apart in his hands. "You've just broken the master if he was in there!"

'Suddenly a voice drifted in a perfect line of wings from

the back of the crowd. A young boy walked forward, his finger pointed to what Mathilde and Torson would normally have called the sky.

'The young boy said, "The master speaks from bushes or from the tops of mountains only. I have no knowledge of instructions given from dung."

'Everyone was impressed with his opinion. Everyone waited for someone else to make the move. The boy spoke again: "And who among you can see a mountain?"

'Everyone looked. Only small hills.

'"Then there must be a burning bush somewhere," flew a sentence. "There! Look!"

'From the slope, a rabbit ran from a bush, and a group broke off and surrounded the bush. They asked why it did not address them. One of them set it on fire to get it talking. But the bush burned away without a word.

'"Any statues around?" asked a woman from another section of the crowd. "He's most likely to talk to us from a statue." A few broke away to search for statues. Others said they'd find a mountain. Had to be one somewhere.

'They returned with nothing, exhausted, confused, some wringing their hands. An argument blew up between a red-haired boy and the young, serious boy about how to address objects that might contain the master. The argument made the crowd divide along the lines of their ideas. Some said that people hadn't addressed the dung properly: the order of words used was incorrect, that the speakers should have tried combinations of words, for instance, "Oh, Master!" at the end, not the beginning.

'Others maintained that the master could only appear on a mountain, but since there wasn't one, they'd have to wait until one formed.

'The third group refused to go along with either of the first two. A mountain? No! Only a statue.

'From that split came another split, and from that split a splinter group left to find the master. And they left, rebuking the addressors of dung, the statue seekers, and the burners.'

'Rebuking?' asked the child.

'Correcting. Anyway, things got worse. Some couldn't decide which group to belong to and ran wildly from one to another and suggested they connect together the best bits of all the ideas so that they'd get something right, no matter what the truth was. Soon white figures criss-crossed the valley floor.

'Mathilde and Torson watched all this for a while and then grew weary. They felt bored and this was only their first day in heaven. Both lay down until their eyes closed. After a while, Torson woke to a mild tremor on the ground. He said to Mathilde, "Stop shaking, will you?"

'But the tremor did not stop, and he moved to wake Mathilde from her bad dream or whatever made her move around so much. But she was already awake. She pointed to the ground, worried. People stood around. No one seemed to know what was happening.'

'And what then?' asked the child.

'Slowly, the tremor became deep thunder.

'Torson said, "Someone important is coming."

'Manes distorted the hill line. A line of buffalo crested the top and swept down the hill, followed by more. And more. Thousands of the beasts.

'Those resident the longest forced their way to the front.

'And they saw wings slip from the hooves, so they knew the buffalo were speaking. The more experienced readers watched intently the patterns of wing flight.

'"What are they saying?" a resident of nine years said. The readers did not answer immediately but turned to each other in great anxiety.

'"What are the buffalo saying?"

'The chief reader's voice shook as though tossed about in a fierce wind. "They are saying, *Good evening, Christians!*"

'And he turned and fought through the assembled brethren, his face paler than light. And the beasts charged like a rhythmical blast, and the light moved aside and the sky went black, and the buffaloes' eyes shone in the night, and they rolled over the residents of the valley as well as Mathilde and Torson at the rear of the crowd, the last to be battered under the hooves.'

'"Must not be heaven," said Torson to Mathilde as they fell under the beasts.

'"What?" Mathilde said.

'"I don't know. What did I just say?" asked Torson.

'"I thought I heard you say something."'

I said, 'And that is the end of the tale of heaven.'

'That's a strange fairy tale,' the teacher said.

'How did I do?' I said.

'It's like something I would have invented,' he said.

Surprised, that's what he was. He didn't think I had it in me. Now I had him thinking, *Is the baker really as stupid as he looks and talks? Is it an act? Is he a human after all, not the monster everyone thinks he is? Can the terrible rumours be untrue, after all?*

THE THIRD TRUCK

The third truck had pulled up to the gate. As before, the tailgate lowered, the bodies jumped out. Fewer passengers this time, maybe ten. They trooped across the short distance to where the first two groups waited. I tried to see if I knew any of them but it was impossible. From where I stood, though, they did seem better dressed because they didn't flap their arms around or blow into their hands. And I didn't see them welcomed the way the second group had been.

A List of Inventions

He pointed down to the hole.

'Dig.'

I jumped in and dug and thought about inventions because they were something to think about. I had learned about them from books and now they brought back the calmness of the quiet evenings I spent in study. Stacks of them. I couldn't get enough information. So as a means to pass time and doubt, I remembered.

You can still breathe the exact air men breathed thousands of years before Buddha. Go to Newfoundland or north of that place. Take a boat to the icebergs and cut off a few small pieces from the water-level layer, because that ice is thousands of years old. Drop the pieces into a glass of water and watch the bubbles rise to the surface. That is air trapped in layers when the snow fell all that time ago. You can breathe that air if you bend to the glass and hold a towel over your head. You can be the first man in a million years to do it. The great natural time machine.

That's not an invention but an insight of my own.

The first known reference to parachutes occurs in 90 BC, in Jsuma Ch'ien's *Historical Records*. I can't remember what they jumped from, but their legs dangled in space and that's what counts, isn't it?

The scientist Win Hu tied forty-seven gunpowdered rockets to his chair in an effort to make a flying machine in the early 1500s; they blew up and blew him up.

Cornelius Drebbel designed and built a submarine that in 1620 carried twenty-four people propelled by a crew that rowed fifteen feet below the surface of the Thames. He never revealed how he got the sailors to breathe. But since they didn't die, they did breathe, probably with the use of saltpetre.

Gold was used to fill teeth in the early 1400s.

Anaximander of Miletus in around 550 BC produced the first known map of the earth on a cylinder. Sailors in open waters could see the bend of the earth from the decks of their ships.

In 1936 pottery jars lined with copper and the remains of iron bars were found in Baghdad. They date from around 230 BC and are the earliest discovered electric batteries.

The first building erected by Puritans in America was a brewery. They ran out of beer on the voyage to Virginia; so they stopped at Plymouth Rock. Plymouth Rock Brewery. Ah, isn't life great all the same?

You can't know enough of this stuff. Information, I mean.

I called to the teacher, 'Tell you what.'

'Yes?'

'Let's find out what you know. Just for the fun of it.'

The teacher drew his coat closer to him and turned up the collar. 'But you are the object of interest today, my friend. I really want to get inside that head of yours.'

'In time. You first,' I said.

'Okay. What do you want to know?'

I spirited my mind to my desk at home, opened the books.

'When did the first plane land on a US aircraft carrier?'

'Don't know,' he said.

'A model 39-B on the USS *Langley* in 1922.'

I tried another: 'When did the first Japanese invasion of America happen?'

'Don't know really. Didn't they invade the Aleutians in World War II?'

'The story is that around 2640 BC a junk sailed thousands of miles east from Japan and came to a gigantic land mass. Captained by Xi and He. The legend dates from the sixth century BC.'

He said, 'People then were just as ingenious as they are now. It's all been done before. What's important is what people understood, not dates.'

'Dates are important,' I said.

He shoved his hands into his pockets, leaving the cigarette on his lips. 'Why?'

'In 1492 America was discovered by Columbus,' I said.

He laughed. 'And I discovered the men's toilet in a hotel last week. I came across it. I saw it. I went back to my friends in the lobby who were downing martinis and said, "I found the toilet."'

'I don't like that talk.'

'I don't either. Maybe I feel uneasy saying these things hundreds of years after they can't defend themselves. They got hungry, fell in love too. Saying these things so long after the fact, it's too certain of itself, too right somehow.'

'You're right, *right* may not exist. When was the first Viking raid on Britain?'

'June 8, 793,' he said.

'I'm impressed,' I said.

'Don't be. Taught it last week. It's still in my mind, that's all.'

'One answer right. Some teacher of history you are. I know more than you do.'

'You and every fly-by-nighter like you can spout off as long as you want.'

I ignored his taunt. 'Everything that happened, happened, and it happened. That's the news.'

'I don't trust the news,' he said.

'You are a doubting Thomas, then.'

'I doubt Thomas doubted, but I hope he had the courage to.'

'Maybe you and I aren't all that far apart,' I said.

He shook his head, stared.

'You and I, Baker, are not of the same species. We are farther apart than the distance between the sun and one inch from the end of the circle around the universe that would bring you back to the sun.'

'So we're not that far apart.'

We glared at each other with as much energy as the conditions allowed. He on his feet up there, I on my feet in the hole. Anything could have happened at that moment.

What happened? We laughed. Briefly. Then a bad blast shook the field itself, it seemed, and sent the trees boiling in their branches. We shuddered against the cold and moaned in the sheer cutting force of it, and then, as quickly, we felt our roles.

I took to the shovel and swore at my bad luck.

BIBLE WRITING CLASS

'Two fifty-five p.m. and all is well!' the teacher shouted in a mock town crier mode.

The whisky had warmed me up a little, which was no good now that I'd be cool in the extremities. Frostbite a real possibility. The teacher's fingers must be sticks of frozen steak, I thought.

The hole was darker than the field and I couldn't locate the pickaxe for a moment. A sheen of snow had covered it in the fifteen minutes I was topside. I stood and held my palm to my forehead. One and a half metres deep for sure. Half a metre more to go, maybe an hour, depending on the ground.

'We're running late,' I said. 'It'll be an hour.'

If he heard me, he paid no attention. He did not respond when he didn't want to. I found that infuriating. Who the hell did he think he was?

'I wrote a play once,' said the teacher. 'A one-act, one-scene play. You won't like it.'

He seemed animated. For a while there I thought he was gone under. Pneumonia, hypothermia, the works.

I said, 'And just because I told you a fairy story, now I have to hear your play.'

'Right.'

'That's fine, Teacher, do your play, but I will not act out anything like my brother had to do in your class. Not now and not in a million years.' I punctuated my statement with the point of the pickaxe under a rock.

He said, 'My play is entitled, "The Day the Count Went Wrong in the New Testament Writing Room".'

'In other words, it's called "Blasphemy",' I said. 'I can't hear this.'

'The play lasts two minutes,' he said. 'I'll just speak it. Listen.'

Setting: *By candlelight on a wooden desk in a small room, a scribe transcribes the beginning of St Matthew's gospel. He carefully writes out the names of the progeny and descendants of Abraham, as instructed. He speaks out loud as he writes. A monk enters and stands silently behind him.*

SCRIBE: . . . and Phares begat Esrom; and Esrom begat Aram; and Aram begat Aminadab; and Aminadab begat Naasson; and Naasson forgot Salmon; and Salmon did that to Booz's mother; and Booze begat Obed; and Obed begat Jesse . . .

MONK: What are you saying? Is that what you wrote? Back there. Here! [*He points.*]

SCRIBE [*despairingly*]:   What? What is it now?

MONK: You have to use the correct word for that. It's 'begat.' Declined, it is 'bego, begas, begat, begamus, begit, begit'. You are required only to use the third person singular form of the verb, and you can't even get that right!

SCRIBE: Begas?

MONK [*shouting*]:   That's not funny!

SCRIBE: Look, I'm losing my mind here! All those names from antiquity. On and on and on.

MONK: We have to establish an unbroken link. Otherwise there's a gap. A missing link.

SCRIBE [*resigned*]:   How many more names?

MONK: Each one represents about thirty years, so we'd need, let's see, you've got this many so far, that's good, yes. [*Sternly*] Scribe, you need another thirty-seven names.

SCRIBE: No! I can't. Can't I just say 'Josaphat 1' and 'Josapaht 2'?

MONK [*hands on hips*]:   You'll do no such thing. They all have to be materially different in character; otherwise the list is tainted by suspicion of faulty transcription.

Leaves the room

The scribe goes into a state of panic and hyperventilates. He commits suicide in a horrible manner. Enter again the monk, who places a sign on the front window of the transcribing room: WANTED, SCRIBE, NEW/OLD TESTAMENT.

'The end!' said the teacher. 'What did you think?'

'I think it is a piece of nastiness unparalleled in the history of modern theatre.' (I had read that statement somewhere and it came to mind in the nick of time.)

'Dig,' he said.

I hadn't waited. Already swinging.

A Dialogue About
Who Made What

'It doesn't have to be exactly two metres deep, you know,' the teacher said. 'As long as you get the dimensions approximately correct, you can signal to the soldiers that you've got it done.'

'Why should I signal to them?'

'They won't move out of that enclosure until they know they have to. When you finish, you signal them with a torch.' He took a tube out of his pocket.

I said, 'Okay.' He made sense for once. And it wasn't a gun, at least.

The wind settled a bit and the teacher poured a little whisky onto his palms and rubbed the alcohol over his face in brisk circles. Then he put his hand on his chin.

'Look, Baker, people have tried to figure out how the world originated for thousands of years.'

I said, 'I do too sometimes, when I'm mixing an apple pie in the shop before I open for business.'

'Aristotle—'

'Who?'

'The Greek. Aristotle said that history is particular, someone did this or had this done to him; poetry, however, illustrates what might have been. It brings forward knowledge from the unconscious memory. It fills out the spaces and makes them real.'

'What use is that?'

'If we know how we really were, we know what we really are.'

'That's very well,' I said. 'But I have a question for you: were we made this way? Have we always been this way? Will we ever change?' And I gathered myself for the damning question: 'Which, Teacher, do you believe in: evolution or creation?'

'I believe in both.'

'Hey! That's cheating! How can you believe in two opposing ideas?'

'They aren't.' He sighed, 'Look, the deserts of the earth are littered with bones tens of millions of years old. I also think that humans were created, and we've been around for millions of years, but the evidence has been destroyed by climate change, volcanic eruptions, earthquakes.'

'Time couldn't get rid of that kind of evidence.'

'Really? Okay, name me three religions older than six thousand years.'

'That's nonsense!'

'Name me three buildings older than fifteen thousand years. Things don't survive, my friend. Earthquakes, fire. Libraries burn. Skeletons fall apart. Information goes up in smoke or out with the electricity. Our history is measured by the fact that we don't have much of it.'

As I watched the teacher, I thought, *what a sight to behold.* He had entered his preachy mode, the one my brother described often to me. A voice like a preacher, arms in the air, froth at his lips.

I didn't want him to lose control and do something stupid.

I said, 'Perhaps there's not much history because the world was created in one go, you know, the seven days and all that.'

'Oh for the love of Jesus, if you believe that you'll believe anything.'

He pressed his hand against his forehead like a man suddenly under stress.

'You should read Archbishop James Ussher then. You'll like him. In 1654 he wrote that the world was created on 26 October 4004 BC, at nine a.m.'

I said, 'That's entirely possible.'

'And the dinosaur bones that are seventy million years old?'

'Maybe God put them there as a test.'

'What? What?'

My attempt to calm him had failed. He shouted into a crescendo:

'The only test, Baker, is how not to erase ourselves from the map. Our history is that things don't last. Every generation creates the right monsters to destroy itself.'

I'd had enough. 'And the source of my deafness is in your voice. I hate it when you preach. You do go on.'

'Then I'll shut up.'

He pointed. 'Dig, Baker. I want that thing dug and I want it dug now!'

We didn't speak for a few minutes, in part because I'd hit a rocky patch with the shovel and had to lean in heavily on the cusp of the steel, which left me short of breath and irritable. When I looked up, he stared at the ground as if in conversation with it.

I said, 'Don't you believe in anything? Don't you stand squarely for anything? All your fancy talk.'

'I believe that the Greek Thales said the world rested on water.'

'Of course the man said that. It was everywhere he looked.'

'And Heraclitus said that reality was a fire of matter, always in chaos. What we'd now call atoms pulverize each other to make what appears to be solid matter. Scientifically, he was right, though he used the language of poetry.'

'Of course.'

'The Greeks believed the earth was a sphere and the sky a rotating sphere that contained the stars, moon, and sun. They could see the earth was curved and they could see the stars and moon and planets rotating. Aristotle said that the sky contained fifty-five spheres with the heavenly bodies set in ether.'

'Got a bit lost in the poetry there, didn't he?' It was all I could say. I hadn't a clue what he talked about and it didn't seem to me to be that important to anyone but him.

He continued, 'The Egyptians believed that the God of Air held up the dome of the sky. The Sun-God Ra sailed across the heavens, under the sea, and back up the next day. Their calendars were perfect to the minute.'

'I accept that. This means they had a way to certainty. They measured things, observed, made calculations. But poetry?'

'Plato took care of poetry. He was the first Greek, along with Socrates, to claim that a real world lay outside this world. Not to trust what you saw around you. The real world lay somewhere up there.' The teacher pointed skyward.

I looked up. I liked the *not trusting* bit.

The teacher said, 'Plato said we live in a cave with a fire behind us, and we glimpse shadows on the cave wall we call the truth but never the real sun, and few are brave enough to leave the cave; and if one does, he'll be unable to see properly when he returns to the cave because the brightness of the sun has blinded him, and people will forbid anyone else to leave, thinking the outside dangerous.'

'I believe Plato meant heaven,' I said.

'In a way, he did. He said that every object in the world was a poor copy of a purer thing that existed elsewhere.'

'Of course.'

'You could say that all things in nature are reflected or reflect other things: the moon the sun, the water the moon, the window the water, the glass bowl the window, the eye the glass, the eye another eye. But he meant things in particular. That the tree was a copy of the form of a pure tree. That's why Plato hated painting. For him, it represented a copy of a copy of the original.'

'So he'd have hated even more a photograph of someone painting a tree.'

'Yes, that would be a copy of a copy of a copy of the original.'

'Or a poem about someone taking that photograph.'

'That would be a copy of a copy of a copy of a copy of the original.'

What I said next came from nowhere. 'No,' I said, 'that would be Plato on sedatives.'

He watched me for a moment and then laughed.

'That's got a nice ring to it, Baker. *Plato on sedatives*. Could be a college rock band. Maybe you have a bit of the poet in you after all.'

And when he smiled at me, I saw the creases line the corner of his eyes.

Six Lines

A whistle. Then another. I looked up. I was safe in the hole, but the wind cut the air above my head into slices, so I popped my head up a few times to get the picture. The soldier at the gate blew a whistle, pointed repeatedly to a spot in the field. The scene with the crowd looked like a soccer match after a bad foul with everyone crowded around the injured player. But in a soccer match the players don't assemble into six lines, and if they did, they'd do it a lot quicker than this bunch. The crowd shuffled into six huddled thin lines. The gate soldier went back to the gate.

Closer to us, the soldiers in the gun emplacement didn't react to the movements at all. More tea, more wood on the fire.

And above me, at the edge of the hole, ever higher, the teacher.

With a question.

LIVE ON THE
KHAN CONNECTION

'Baker, what's the best thing you've learned?'

I dug fast to stay warm. I could no longer wonder how the teacher managed the cold.

'When I learned about the great Mongol leaders.' I had to shout everything.

'Of course!'

'And I practised news reports from the massacre sites, just so I'd feel I was there.'

'Of course!'

'Are you laughing at me?'

'Of course!'

To an onlooker, the teacher and I were two people shouting at each other in a field in a winter storm. One of them visible, the other in a hole. The proof of the one in the hole? A shovel and pickaxe head appearing at regular intervals.

'Let's hear about the Mongols,' the teacher said. 'We have time.'

I said, 'I call it The Khan Connection.'

He asked, 'Is your microphone plugged in?'

'What on earth—? Oh, yes, I have power, yes.'

'Good. You can begin,' he said.

I held the shovel handle to my mouth and addressed the

sky a few centimetres to the right of the teacher's head. I adopted the tone of an informed, intelligent, serious, committed, earnest newsreader.

'Thank you for watching Eastern European Television's morning news on this troubled day in the year 1241. We have a report from the latest in a series of incidents relating to the Mongols, an obscure band of nomads who have terrorized the civilized world.

'Now, a warning. Parts of this report are shocking and may upset sensitive viewers.

'The catalogue of terrors these savages have perpetrated is, according to some, a signal that the end of Christendom is near. Recently, in 1238 or thereabouts, Matthew Paris, a monk of St Albans, one of the finest reporters of our age, described the fierce horsemen who rolled from the east through the Carpathian mountain passes and into eastern and central Europe, burning, raping, and slaughtering every living thing: people, pets, trees, and plants. They levelled the walls of cities and left nothing but wind and thousands of corpses that littered the area for years. In a raid on Baghdad, they killed between one and two million and left them where they fell in the heat.'

I lowered the microphone and coughed to clear my throat.

The teacher spoke with a hand over his mouth, 'Wait, Baker, is this you talking?'

'No,' I said. 'This is a news report from medieval Europe. Haven't you been listening? Can't you let me broadcast it?'

'Yes.'

'Good morning again, viewers. Let's go to Matthew Paris, standing by the scene of the alleged massacres. Sorry, I mean, reporting from outside his abbey in England.'

I moved to my left.

'Thank you,' I said in an English accent. 'Matthew Paris here. In order to put this in context for your viewers, let me quote from the Muslims in the East: "a monstrous and inhuman race have burst forth from the northern mountains".

'Thank you, Matthew. Is it true that our enemies the Saracens actually asked assistance from the King of England, writing that nothing would soon stand between the Mongols and us?

'I believe so—

'But what kind of devastation do these so-called Tartars or Mongols practise? What has made these Saracens so scared?

'The Mongols eat their victims. Heathens, at our doorstep without warning. There is a very real possibility that these invaders will appear in Rome any time now and lay it to waste. Their scouts have been sighted at the outskirts of Vienna and about a hundred miles from Venice. Venice!'

The teacher shouted, 'The wind! I can't hear you!'

I let Matthew Paris continue his report without interruption.

'They are at our door. They have destroyed two great Christian armies, at Leignitz and Mohi, the best of our French and Hungarian mounted cavalry, and split Europe, decimating our forces, everything we throw at them.

'Matthew, sorry to interrupt, but for a local perspective, let's go now to a witness to the battle at Leignitz who is standing outside the ruins of his home. What is your name, sir?

'I am a miller.

'Mr Miller, what did you see at Leignitz? We hear conflicting accounts. Some say the Europeans put up a good fight, others claim dirty tricks by the Mongols.

'On the way to Leignitz the Mongols stormed our town and burned it to the ground. We retreated to the city fortress, that's how we survived. The Tartars were in too much of a hurry to bother. We were lucky.

'Mr Miller, what happened at Leignitz? Were you there?

'I followed them to Leignitz, far behind, keeping downwind of their rearguard. I felt that God had spared me to be a witness to the destruction of our Christian way of life. Nothing could have prepared me for what I saw.

'And what did you see at Leignitz? How many rode to meet the Mongol armies?

'Numbers of men? I think there was a splendid army of our best men, as far as the eye could see, covering hills and plains with their wagons and geese and cows.

'Hello? This is Matthew Paris again, can you hear me?

'Yes, we can all hear you.

'Sorry to interrupt Mr Miller while he's telling you what happened, but I did the research. I have the numbers.

'Go ahead, Matthew Paris.

'Russia was gone, overrun. The Mongols advanced into Poland, where a local duke, Henry, desperately assembled a fighting force of about thirty thousand men, including Teutonic Knights, the heaviest armoured fighting men in the Christian world.

'The Mongol generals advanced twenty thousand men toward the Polish forces, burning Mr Miller's town on the way. They reached Henry's army on 9 April.

'The place, Leignitz, in western Poland.

'On the day of battle, the Mongol generals ordered suicide corps to ride against the Europeans and provoke them into leaving their positions. The Polish archers opened up and the Mongols retreated. Then Henry made the same mistake countless leaders had made – he sent his cavalry after them, the whole knightly tradition of Europe in full battle dress thundering in one gallop after the lightly armed savages.

'Matthew Paris, thank you. Let's get back to Mr Miller, who saw the event unfold. Mr Miller?

'Yes.

'Please recount what you saw the day Europe was brought to its knees.

'I don't have numbers but I saw numbers. I was on a hill under a tree on my hands and knees in terror. I heard nothing, too far away for that. Saw men falling. Saw arrows move through the air like small silver fish crowding a stream. Strange, so much killing and yet silent. It's like, well—

'Yes?

'It's as if it were all something in a vision, silent, something from a long time ago. I felt strange.

'But you told us you were there.

'I was, I was! The Mongols laid smoke and their archers shot into the cavalry's bright reds, their flags, their thunderous gallop. The arrows fell from a great distance on those knights. Everything in a fog: dust and arrows and horses and men falling. The Christians tried to attack into the smoke. The savages moved around and attacked the infantry. Slaughter! And the Mongols sent in their heavy cavalry at a slow trot, then a canter, then a full gallop, screaming. I could only gasp at the bravery of the Europeans. They met the charge head-on. I think maybe it was desperation at death, not courage. The sound of heavy horse slicing into each other should have filled the world. But the sound of the world was somewhere else that day for me. Many Mongols fell as they fought one-to-one. Later I saw the Mongols carrying a head on a spear. Someone said it was a royal head. I ran then, for days I think, back to the fortress in my town, thanking God for my salvation. The Tartars are true to their name. They come from hell.

'Indeed. Thank you for a local view of this tragedy. Please get back to salvaging your belongings. We know how important that must be for you.

'Okay, let's return now to Matthew Paris. Are you there, Matthew? St Albans, do we have you?

'Yes, I can hear you, but as I've said the weather is worsening, that's why my voice is raised. The head on the spear was the Duke Henry's, by the way, and I know that even though I wasn't there.

'No one questions your accuracy, Matthew Paris.

'I do have the numbers, you see. After the battle Mr Miller just described, the savages cut an ear off every corpse and filled nine large sacks with them. At Mohi, two days later, the Mongols slew sixty thousand professional Hungarian soldiers in one battle. Nothing stops their arrows. Repeat: we have no answer to their arrows, which they can shoot while riding. Our knights wear too much armour to match their movements. Their leader Batu has said, "We live in tents, you live in houses and cities. You cannot flee so well."

'The end of the world may indeed finally be at hand. We took these people for granted. We did not realize that a nation of less than a million and a half could conquer and kill forty times their number. They defeated China, Russia, Persia, yet have never colonized the land they conquer. They simply make the greatest cities disappear. Now they are at our doorstep, an apocalypse, the four horsemen. That Mongol general, Batu, will reach the Atlantic inside the year. Our Christian kings have said their goodbyes. Our way of life is about to vanish from the face of the earth. Death will come hard for us. They bury their prisoners upside down in the ground, hands tied behind their backs, they skin them alive, they roll them in carpets and throw them into rivers, crush them with stones, truss them and shoot them, rape the women—'

'Can I ask Matthew a question?' said the teacher.

'Yes, the teacher has a question, Matthew.

'Go ahead, but quickly. It's getting bad here. We're promised more snow by this afternoon.'

'Matthew, have you ever actually seen a Mongol?' the teacher asked.

'No, not exactly.'

'Not one?'

'No.'

'And you've lived in England most of your life?'

'This is Matthew Paris, signing off from St Albans.

'That completes our coverage of the Mongol invasion of Europe.'

The teacher applauded, though I suspected he was merely clapping to keep himself warm rather than to congratulate me.

I said, 'You hit a weak spot with those questions for Matthew Paris.'

'An interesting story, Baker. You know your history. All the bloody stuff, anyway.'

'I know everything I need to know,' I said.

SNOW

Snow lands silently like a soft white magnet that arrives in pieces and builds its strength as the inches gather. Snow is a magnet, and the first thing snow attracts is the ordinary noise of the country. The magnet sucks it all in and silences the air for miles. The next things the magnet drags in are your steps. They get heavier until you plod and have to pull your leg up to make the next step, which means that your eyes are drawn down by the magnet too. Then the magnet reaches for the parts of itself that landed on the trees. Branches splinter and fall. Next to descend are the clouds, low and bursting with grey; they loom and scud along the fields and fences and roads and mailboxes. The last thing the magnet attracts is direction. You can see everyone's and everything's footsteps. You know where they've been and you know where they've gone. You can follow them if you want.

Snow never pulled anything from me. And I walk in others' footsteps so I don't leave my own. That's my theory of snow.

A Dialogue about Nimrod

The teacher rubbed his chin. 'You know,' he said, 'the Mongol arrow reminds me of the ancient tale of Nimrod.'

'Nimrod is a name I haven't heard before. What's this, a trick?'

'No,' he said. 'Nimrod was a great hunter from the Steppes who claimed dominion over the world because he had shot an arrow into the sky and hit God.'

'What?'

'Lucky shot, probably. Nimrod shot it into the sky, which was a kind of custom, and next thing there's blood pouring down. He presumed he had shot God.'

I said, 'Imagine God's surprise.'

'You're telling me.'

I said, 'One minute you're in charge and the next you've got an arrow in the back, falling to earth, and fast.'

The teacher said, 'No, if we stay with that train of thought, we go astray. No record of God actually falling. If it were you, for instance, what would you do? Probably hold on with your fingertips and look down at the human ants. And in the distance you can see all the people of the world, all the continents, turning slowly beneath you, and you realize it was all yours and an arrow ended it. One lousy arrow.'

'The one with your name on it. Jesus,' I said.

He said, 'I've read that some general once remarked, "I'm not afraid of the arrow with my name on it. What I fear are the hundreds of arrows falling with no name on them."'

I said, 'But this was a rising arrow.'

'That's right.'

'So what happened to Nimrod?'

The teacher said, 'God didn't die. He gave Nimrod a nasty disease, killed him.'

I clapped my hands.

'It's just a metaphor, Baker. It didn't actually happen.'

'How do you know? Were you there?'

He said, 'I don't know and I wasn't there.'

'So where did the blood come from then? These buckets of blood on the ground? Answer that one!'

The teacher smiled weakly at me. 'Well, maybe it was spilled wine. Maybe the gods were laughing too hard at that story to hold their drinks steady. One arrow shot into the wide-open heavens and hitting God? I mean, come on!'

'You're a secret heathen, Teacher, that's your one huge fault. What I mean by that is that every other fault you have stems from that one.'

The teacher raised his hand in a mock salute. 'Thank you, I drink to your god. Good luck to him, that's what I say. Now tell me more stories of the Mongols.' And he coughed, twice, three times.

He looked thirsty to me, worn out. Maybe the effort at humour stretched his resources. But we were playing this to the end.

I said, 'The Mongols never occupied a city they defeated. Simply rode on. They bluffed everyone.'

'Bluff, you say?'

'Cruelty and military instinct. They rode along the bank of the Danube with children impaled on their lances to give the Hungarians a taste of what was to come. They wore leather armour, and underneath a silk tunic that wrapped around the head of an arrow that entered the flesh with it, making the arrow easy to pull out, for it is on the way out of the body that arrows cause much of their damage. Their own arrows had slit ends so narrow that they were useless in European bowstrings, and those arrows meant certain death. Friar Longjumeau described the miles of bones that littered the roads along the Mongol path of war.'

'Tell me they had a culture aside from war,' the teacher said.

'They never harmed an ambassador, apart from one man who wouldn't shut up as they escorted him through the country. Him, they dragged out of his carriage and kicked to a pulp. Others were safe.

'On 7 May 1253, Friar William Rubruck took the road east to meet the great Khan Mangu with letters from King Louis IX in his pocket. The Friar reached Karakorum, the Mongol capital, seven months later.

'Rubruck suffered from the constant frigid weather "so intense it split stones and trees". They travelled weeks without a sight of towns or another human being. He wrote in *A Journey to the Eastern Parts of the World* that the Khan Mangu, out of compassion, allowed him to remain in his camp until the abominable weather was over. He said to Rubruck, *We believe that there is only one God, by whom we live and by whom we die . . . But as God gives to the hand different fingers, so He has given to men diverse ways of Himself. To you Christians he has given the Holy Scriptures; and you do not keep them.*

'Over four months at the court of the great Khan, Rubruck learned from a Tibetan monk about life behind the Great Wall of China. The monk described a thing called paper money that the Chinese used and the system of writing images that represented words: "They write with a brush such as painters paint with, and they make in one figure the several letters containing a whole word."

'He said the Mongol capital was no bigger than a small French town, but like nothing he had ever seen, divided into quarters, each containing people with particular skills: jewellers from France, scientists from Persia and China, a block of European artists, twelve Buddhist temples, two mosques, and a Christian church at the very end of town. He wrote, "The inhabitants are very fine craftsmen in every art, and their physicians know a great deal about the power of herbs and diagnose very cleverly from the pulse." Mangu Khan arranged for the Friar to debate the Buddhists as he and the members of the Mongol court got drunk.'

Room for a
Conspiracy Theory

'Baker, how in heaven's name did you remember all this stuff?'

'Years of lonely reading. I have read more on the subject, Teacher, than you can imagine. I have kept my ear to the ground. I have access to rare documents unavailable to others.'

'Really?' the teacher said with arched eyebrows.

'The Mongols could shoot while they rode. Who taught them to do that? Answer me that? Rituals. I have proof of strange lights in the sky described by writers of the time.'

'Really?' the teacher said.

'How else could a puny nation take over a third of the known world? How else could they go from not even being a nation and never having been heard of before to attacking and defeating four major civilizations in fifty years? All those claims: good battle tactics, patience, surprise, speed, their arrows, their ability to cross great distances and still fight effectively – I don't buy them.'

'Is this history or some fantasy of yours?'

'What's the difference? In the Old Testament it says, the book of Exodus I'm talking about, that God took his people out of Egypt and into remote places where they could live without corruption. Some Christians left western Europe.

Their descendants now live in a remote valley in China, waiting for the year 2150, the millennium of the end of the Dark Ages, when they will challenge the West. A great army of disease.'

'Disease?'

'If you count all the minutes since the dark ages and multiply them by six times the length of time it took God to create the earth and divide it by the number of verses in Deut. 5:27, you'll have the exact number that will spill over the Western borders without warning. That's what I've read. Just like the Mongols. The hordes will be microbes, AIDS and everything, doing their horrible work in the dead of night. People falling like flies.'

'This is madness. I'm sorry I asked.'

'And it all began with Genghis Khan.'

It All Began With Genghis Khan

'Genghis Khan?' The teacher's eyes widened. 'Did you say Genghis Khan? You know of him?'

'I have studied his ways for over a year. I have read every book in the library that bears his name, even on a single page.'

'Then answer me this: who was more evil, Mr Fievez or Genghis Khan?'

I smiled, 'The books I have gathered on him!'

The teacher took some rocks and made two piles.

'These are skulls,' he said. 'This is Genghis Khan's pile. Each rock is four million people. This is Fievez's pile. Each rock is one hundred people. Same amount of rocks on each side. Who is more evil?'

'Be careful,' I said. 'The rocks might fall into the hole and I'll have to lift them out again.'

'If they fall in, I'll help you. Now to my question. Your answer, please.'

I answered, 'Genghis Khan became active militarily in the early 1200s and killed close to one-fifth of the world's known population, about twenty million.'

'Then my question is an easy one. Mr Khan or Mr Fievez?'

'It's not an easy one. Fievez wasn't in charge. Khan was a leader.'

'Mr Khan, then?'

'No, I didn't say that, did I? Different time. And where's all the evidence of evil? Maybe what he did was the right thing for the time. How do we know? What was he thinking? What were his motives?'

He said, 'So we just have the numbers, the body count?'

'And the strategies.' The teacher irritated me with those quick questions.

He said, 'The strategies of the late, great Mr Khan will now be discussed by the learned Baker who is standing in a hole on the coldest day in memory in the farthest corner of earth's imagined corners!'

'Go to hell,' I said. 'Go to hell and just go to hell.'

He said, 'Are we not there already?'

'Nowhere near it. It's too cold in this field.'

'It's too cold,' he shouted. 'We must be nowhere near hell then!'

'Shut up,' I said. 'Shut your mouth or they'll come over to me!'

The teacher turned to the soldiers stationed at the edge of the field.

'I doubt that Mr Khan will attract any of them,' he said.

'Jump in and we'll talk.' I was desperate to keep him quiet.

'Let's do it from here,' he said. 'I'll stay where I am, you stay in the hole.'

'What are we doing?' I asked.

'I know something of Khan,' he said. 'I spent a class day teaching the exploits of the Mongol leader. Presumably your brother went home and—'

'—told me, yes. He came home excited about the twenty million. I couldn't believe it. We figured it out together with pencil and paper, twenty million by one and a half metres (average height) is thirty-five million metres, is thirty thousand kilometres of corpses laid end to end. It wasn't in a school history book so I went to the library. I think it was Khan who first made me want to read. I have him to thank.'

He said, 'Khan wouldn't care much for your thanks. He had an army faster and better than any other at the time. That's how you win. He didn't defeat, he obliterated.'

I said, 'You don't have to watch for long knives that way. No vengeful relatives. No relatives' dogs, no plants managing to grow in the ruins. He erased cities. He put the wind back in charge with nothing to oppose its flow across the land.'

I really liked the sound of what I'd said.

'So who'll be Khan in our play?' the teacher asked me.

'This isn't your classroom.'

'Oh, come on. Look, you can be the Khan.'

I said, 'You will not match my wits on this subject.'

'Then we should keep it short lest you take the advantage over me.' He breathed deeply and closed his eyes. 'Let's begin, shall we?'

ALL MY FRIENDS
GOT MARRIED

The weather worsened. Maybe I thought that because it was getting dark and the sun had stopped whatever little warmth it gave to the field. My fingers, through the gloves, were brittle-blue and sore. I examined the hopelessness of my situation, the point to which all my reading had taken me. *Why not?* I thought. We can play. I'll buy the time for me, for him. Maybe dark will fall and we'll be forgotten. Isn't that the state of being alive? You fall into the light, dark falls, and you get forgotten. You get replaced. Your friends find other friends. They have to live too. The nature of friendship: the strongest and brittlest substance in the world.

I had a friend in school. We walked together around the football field at break. We shared sweets. Comics. Heartache over girls. The first rose bought for a sweetheart. Then we grew up and money mattered and your last name mattered and what your father did mattered. My father was not an important man. We grew until we graduated and suddenly we were seventeen. My best friend found a girl and I didn't. He's married. I'm not.

What's the point in understanding anything more? I lost and they won. I stood on the outside and watched them practise a successful life. It happened. My best friend is now surely very happy, I'm not. He should have waited for me, but that's not for understanding. You have to look at the facts and plan your survival, because no one else will, that's for sure. Raise all the flags you can and hide under them and don't show your face to the world. Agree with everyone. Speak all languages and none. Learn invisibility. Stand for nothing. Learn to live under cardboard in tunnels, breathe secret air, screw the sweet world of romance. Screw it and they can all go to hell. My friends left me all alone. They all left me alone and didn't care. I survived though. I don't need any of that kind of support now. My strength is my indifference. I survived their cruelties.

A Screenplay on the Great Khan

'If we do this,' I said.

'Yes?'

'Who will you be, if I'm the Khan?'

'Everyone he beat.'

'Okay. Then you'll be the Chinese, the Koreans, the Russians, the countries of the Middle East, the east Europeans, and the central Europeans, and everyone in between.'

'Let the games begin,' the teacher said.

'It's a film, not a game.'

'First a news report, now a film?'

'It has to be a film,' I said. 'Otherwise no one would listen to it. A screenplay is best. With behind-the-scenes footage showing the real Khan. Interviews with victims. A personal interview with the Genghis, the G-man.

1. IN THE TENT OF THE GREAT KHAN –
INTERIOR – DAY

An interviewer sits in a tent in front of Genghis Khan. The flap is open and a desert breeze blows the candles intermittently. The interviewer consults his notebook and speaks with a hint of nervousness.

INTERVIEWER: Genghis Khan, I want to quote something you once said.

KHAN: Yes?

INTERVIEWER: You said, 'I have committed many acts of cruelty and had an incalculable number of men killed, never knowing whether what I did was right. But I am indifferent to what people think of me.'

KHAN: You commit to memory what suits you. How can I add anything to that?

INTERVIEWER: Your story.

KHAN: My story is power, the prettiest story in the world. It makes people sing, shout, swing, stamp, red-blooded, carefree, beautiful, savage, strong. We ruled the biggest empire that ever was and can be. Be careful with your words, historian. I can reach from beyond the grave. I can slit your words from your throat if you put false words into mine.

INTERVIEWER (Nods and swallows visibly):   May I read you the beginning of a screenplay I've done on your life?

KHAN: Read me what you think of my life, though I am indifferent.

INTERVIEWER: My screenplay is called 'Khan.'

TITLE SHOT: KHAN

Opening credits. We see the tip of the rising sun at
the edge of the horizon. The year is 1219 AD.
Background information on the political and tribal
situation in the Far East. Location information.

2. THE RUSSIAN STEPPE – EXTERIOR – DAWN

No music, no words, just silence. The sun appears
and a tinge of red forms low in the sky. And from this
meniscus of rising sun emerges the steadily increasing
pounding of heavy cavalry: the Mongol hordes
thunder from the east!

CUT TO

EXT. RIVER BY A MONGOL SETTLEMENT

A river trickles under sunshine, a small Mongol
encampment in the background. Two boys fish side
by side. Mongol horsemen in training ride across the
fields shooting arrows and swinging their sabres, but
the only sound is the water trickling. The boys watch
the horsemen and leave down the fishing poles and
pretend to be cavalry; they engage in mock battle and
wrestle each other to the ground.

CLOSE-UP

One of the boys sees a fishing pole move. He jumps
up and grabs it, tries to haul in the fish. The other
boy shouts.

BOY 1 (on the left):   It's mine! That is my fishing
        pole! (He tries to grab it. The boy on the right
        pushes him away with his free hand.)

BOY 2:   The fish is mine. Be careful of what is
        mine.

BOY 1:   No, you're a cheat! The fish is not yours.
        Give it to me!

The camera pans to the surface of the river and we
see the boys' shadows struggling for possession of
the fishing pole. The boy on the left wrests the pole
away and begins to pull in the fish that has now
broken the surface. The shadow of the second boy
goes off-camera right and returns with an object in
his hands, brings it down on the head of the first
boy.

CUT TO
Blood on the grass. The second boy is walking back
to the encampment alone with the fish. He sings a
song.

3. A MONGOL TENT – INTERIOR – DAY
A woman looks up from her chair on a heavily
decorated red carpet. The boy enters smiling, holding
up the fish.

WOMAN: Temujin! What a beautiful fish!

She beckons him to her and embraces him. Silence.

WOMAN: Where is your brother? Did he catch one
too?

BOY 1:   Shakes his head.

WOMAN: Temujin – go and get your brother and
we will cook and eat the fish.

The boy lets the fish drop. Stares at it. The woman
stares at it momentarily, then him. After a few seconds,
she lifts the tent flap and looks out. The boy watches
the fish, does not move. The woman turns to him.

WOMAN: What have you done with your brother,
Temujin? Have you been fighting again? Answer
me!

4. IN THE TENT OF THE GREAT KHAN – INTERIOR – DAY

INTERVIEWER: At the tender age of twelve, you
killed your half-brother over a fish, didn't you?

KHAN: Why I killed him is irrelevant. What is
important is that my name was Temujin then.

INTERVIEWER: The world knows you as Genghis
Khan.

KHAN: The world knows little of us. Few saw and
reported. They wrote what suited them. The
world will never see the like of us again.

At this point in the screenplay I grew tired of including all the screenplay details, so I whispered, 'Teacher, I'll tell it ordinary from here on.'

He nodded.

'Khan, we will include in the film more about you growing up, then fast forward two decades. You have united the Mongol tribes and made a military power of a tiny population. You defeated the middle kingdom of China. Now you look west. You take over western Mongolia, now called Kazakhstan. You stand at the mighty doorway of the empire of Islam. Beyond that, Europe, the Atlantic.

'A weak, ignorant people who believe they live in the centre of the world. They have much to learn.

'It is 1212. The city, Samarkand, in the country of Khwarezam, a very important city.

'A place you now call Afghanistan and Iran. I do not want war with those people. We can trade with each other. That's what I tell them. They have a large army, four hundred thousand men. The Shah Mohammad rules it. Although he heads a huge army, he has never fought a tactical enemy before, and he believes himself invincible.

'You need the cloth they produce because Mongols don't weave. People who sit, weave. You sleep in tents, you ride horses across large distances, migrating once a year.

'With wind in our hair. Across thousand-mile steppe.

'What do you do to make friends with Shah Mohammed?

'I need the cloth Samarkand produces. I want peace with them. I send emissaries. After all, a man must have something to aim at in life. A good horse, a distant country, a woman's hand, a long view from a high hill, a valley of fruits and shade of trees.

'I said, Your messengers departed with five hundred camels and gold, precious metals, silk, and ivory.

'I say in my letter to the Shah, *I know your power and the vast extent of your empire. I have a great desire to live in peace with you. I shall regard you as my son. You know that my country is an anthill of fighters, and that I have no need to covet further domains. We have an equal interest in promoting trade between our subjects.*

'The Shah's response?

'His border governor steals my gifts and kills my men.

'Your response?

'Patience. I send another emissary, an official of my court. This time with five hundred camels, fur, sable. I respect their people.

'And?

'My men arrive at a frontier town called Otrar. The local governor has most of them butchered and kills the official of my court. Confiscates my gifts.

'A foolish man, this Shah.

'I let it go. You don't understand power. Power is indifference. I send another ambassador, a Muslim.

'Good move. A sign of respect.

'A Muslim whom the Shah beheads. He sends the rest back to me with their heads shaven. Then he reappoints the governor of Otrar, the man who insulted my emissaries.

'And you let this go?

'Three times is enough. In the summer of 1219, I assemble two hundred thousand riders. My four sons and I go to war against the West.

'Yes! That's the opening credit sequence. It begins. They never saw you coming.

'I am tired. Go, return in three hours.'

KILLING

I continued, 'Scene Five. In the tent of Genghis Khan – interior – day. Genghis Khan is seated in different clothes, looking refreshed. His personal guards watch the interviewer's every movement, one hand on their swords. The interviewer says:

'How does the Shah Mohammad defend his empire? His armies vastly outnumber your forces.

'He spreads his army along the entire eastern border. As though we would attack in the same manner! Numbers mean nothing. I head straight for Otrar. It is a walled city, but I have my siege machines from China, ten thousand prisoners to operate them, and the experts to manufacture mortars and rockets with gunpowder.

'Other weapons?

'Massive crossbows that fire huge arrows, catapults that fling boulders high over the walls. My sappers tunnel under the walls, my battering rams bash the gates. They dare not face us in open battle. They retreat to fortified cities.

'The first battle lasts a month. Hand-to-hand fighting.

'We fight our way in. The governor who killed my emissary fights with his men. When we catch him he is brought to me. I have molten silver poured into his eyes and down his throat.

'What now?

'My armies take two large nearby towns. Everyone is killed in the first, their throats opened, except the craftsmen, whom we need. We take slaves in the second.

'The city of Khojend, your next objective.'

The teacher shivered and waved his hands.

'Sorry to interrupt. Look, I'm cold,' he said. 'Let's cut this short.'

'In a hurry?' I said.

'I didn't say that. I said I was cold. Come on, get on with it. Khan, Baker – whoever you are at this moment – you took more towns, executed their inhabitants.'

'I took Nur and Bukhara. The fate of the holy city of Bukhara is still remembered. The defenders escaped, but I spared the inhabitants. I told them, "I am the flail of God. If you had not committed great sins, God would not have sent a punishment like me upon you." Many kill themselves. The city burned to the ground. For years afterwards, no one returned. Thousands of corpses lie on the ground. The smell extends for miles. A shroud of bones. Not a dog barks, not a branch moves. Everyone in the surrounding area moves away. I plant silence as well as defeat. Silence like a great plain across which I send horses, tens of thousands of ghost horses. The vegetation turned to desert. Nothing living remained. I erased the city.'

'The city of Samarkand. Turkish mercenaries defended it. Thousand of years old even in the thirteenth century. Leather workers, goldsmiths, carvers. They produced paper, ceramics.'

'I arrived at the ancient city in the early months of 1220, dressed thousands of prisoners in Mongol clothes and sent them in my front lines to attack the city. The Turks engaged them. My men staged a retreat, turned, and destroyed the charging Turks, and I walked into the city. I killed thirty thousand soldiers and let the inhabitants leave.'

'Next, the city of Urgench, the capital.'

'They resisted. It fell to me after a six-month siege. They knew what would happen. Men, women, children fought us with axes, sticks, fingernails, their curses, their tears. They begged for mercy. We flooded the city and drowned those who hid from us. Nothing remained.'

'This continued, city after city.'

'I summered in Nasaf, then attacked Termez. After a woman swallowed gems to hide them, I had everyone dis-embowelled to recover treasure hidden in this manner.'

'The city of Balkh.'

'An ancient city, three thousand years old. Alexander the Great married Roxanne there. They surrendered on the promise that they would be unharmed, but I killed a great many of them. In 1222 I returned and killed the survivors. This was our way. Seeing us on the horizon meant death. We did not leave anything standing behind us.'

'A Chinese monk reported that dogs barked in empty streets. No human survived in Balkh.'

'We took many more cities. Few survived to rebuild. We made open spaces where they had stood. That is defeat.'

'The city of Nessa resisted,' said the teacher.

'We tied all seventy thousand together and used them for target practice.'

'Your son Tolui—'

'Oh, of course – and the most violent. He disturbed even me.'

'Perpetrated an outrage—'

'He defeated the enemy.'

'—in the city of Merv. He arrived with seventy thousand horsemen, assaulted the city and was driven back. But the governor surrendered on assurances of mercy. Your son did not keep his word.'

'A word is a word. And my son spared four hundred craftsmen and some slaves. It was not all lost to them.'

'But this was a difficult massacre. Some witnesses stopped counting at 1.3 million bodies. Others say only 700,000 were executed.'

'There were many residents in Merv. Tolui divided up the task among the soldiers. Each had to kill between three and four hundred people.'

'In Nishapur, your son disembowelled everyone and searched their insides for jewellery and stacked 1.7 million skulls in three piles, men women and children.'

'Tolui was cruel. I did not give him the Khanship, but what he did was necessary. We could not be followed.'

'In Herat, your army spared all but the mercenaries. Still, the population revolted. You slaughtered them, then hid and waited for survivors to emerge. You killed 1.6 million in all. Not an ear of corn remained. Not a scrap of clothing.'

'The wind wants no obstruction. We do not like walls.'

'You sent soldiers back to Balkh and Merv and slaughtered any who had returned there.'

'I cannot be followed. The slaughter at Merv was necessary.'

'You died in 1227.'

'Near a mountain range by a lake, in a field with no marker on my grave, the soil trodden flat long ago, a long time ago, by horses. Our horses gallop below us in life; in death, upon us. I ordered that anyone who gazed upon my grave be killed.'

'Why?'

'Men are gawkers. They spend their whole lives standing in one place and looking around them, wishing on a star that they could change their destiny.'

'Why did your descendants not invade western Europe?'

'Twenty years after my death, sitting in their saddles in the hills, our reconnaissance troops could see the towers of your precious European cities. A few weeks' march farther the Atlantic lay waiting for us at the end of Europe. And at the moment of your destruction, at that very moment, we turned back. We went home.

'We never returned.'

A Dialogue in the Field and out of the Screenplay

The weather front moved across the sky and left patches of blue tinged with silver edges of clouds, and our faces lit under the unexpected light. For a few moments the field seemed a happy place to be, and above, the sky seemed something *up there* and wide open and deep, so deep you could fall up into it for ever. As a child I'd thought of the night sky as something under me that I could fall down into through the stars. But I grew older and afraid of anything that meant down. The light rolled over the snow and passed us at the hole, followed by a heavy grey that hung an inch from the ground. And after that, the snow flew again, and it didn't matter any more whether I thought the sky was up or down.

'What, we're out of the screenplay?' The teacher looked puzzled.

'Yes, all done.'

'Okay, you pass,' he said. 'You pass with flying colours.'

I bowed in acknowledgement of his compliment. 'I know my Khan.'

The teacher knelt down and asked me with great delicacy: 'And what have you understood about him? About his wars?'

'The facts are these, that although he killed many people, he was not evil. He was efficient, a master of his time, a great soldier. I learn from the way he lived.'

The teacher flopped his arms and laughed. 'That's frightful. He should have been disposed of at birth. Dragged out of the womb and a sword stuck in his tiny heart. Someone must have known he was coming. Somewhere, a prophet saw something in the guts of a bird or the whisper from an oracle. No one stopped it.' He struck one fist with the other. 'I sometimes think the world has a death wish.'

'Khan, Mister Teacher, was more than his wars. Excuse me, but I'm not stupid. I've told you that. Maybe you are the one who refuses to see the world as it was. You live by your lecture notes.' (I am proud to state that I made that phrase up on the spot.)

He said, 'Lecture notes? I see twenty million dead bodies over as many years. A generation of killing.'

'What about the Taoist monk that Khan befriended in his last years? Khan asked him for the secret of immortality. When he could not tell him, instead of having him killed, Khan befriended him.'

The teacher said, 'A generation of killing.'

I said, 'Teach your students this: after defeating the Chinese and the Russians, the Mongols routed the Persians, the Syrians; in 1241, they chased the King of Hungary through Yugoslavia on small horses. Their armies, always small. Horses small, men small.'

'And?'

'All of what you know about human nature, they knew. But with one difference, Teacher. The wind, the open Steppe, the outline of an ancient town, some thousands of years old, what they would have done to the Mongols if the

Mongols didn't do it to them. When did you feel like that last? Don't you live the same day, haven't you lived the same day, for all your life?'

'Are you Khan or the Baker? I'm confused. Are we still playing the game?'

'The men the Mongols killed, Chinese, Russians, the countries they killed, paved a huge road through the world, east to west. This is what the Mongols did, through violence.'

'Twenty million bits of violence, Baker Khan.'

I said, 'Marco Polo, the hero of the Christian west. This man travelled freely because of the Mongols. He went from outpost to outpost along roads they made safe, where before he would not have gone ten miles without a knife at his throat, or would have stayed in Venice reading his precious books. That is the fact of the matter. That's what sickens me about your type. You favour the arts, but it was violence that spread those arts.'

The teacher shouted, 'You make me sick!'

'And you're a snob! Read your damn history. Europe before the Mongols. No money, no building, no roads, no reading, no art, no science. Villages in the dark forest. Nothing for hundreds of years until nations had boundaries and soldiers guarded the roads. Then came commerce. Then the drawers and scribblers. The art-people.' I drew in the air. 'It's all down to military power, Teacher. Brute force made your Renaissance, the artists and merchants that plied the Silk Road. When the roads are safe the art crowd come out of the woodwork and open their little shops and buy their canvases. So don't be a snob. Don't bite the hand that feeds you!'

'The Mongols are gone,' the teacher said.

'Wrong. You'll see them if you want to. You can still find the heavy artillery stones that Hulegu's army hauled up the mountain slopes in 1256 to catapult into the Persian town of Alamut; the stones still lie scattered around the ruins.'

'The Mongols are gone,' he said.

WHAT IS A HOLE?

The wind whipped pebbles from the mound of dirt and rocks back into the hole. A tiny stream of them collected at the bottom. If I waited long enough, every ounce I removed would end up back in the hole. Nature doesn't like holes. It fills them with rain, mud, rivers, oceans. Today the field was filled with snow and the sky with wind and our skin with blue-black cold; but all the talking in the world wouldn't fill the silence that was everywhere around us.

The recent battle for the town made me think of holes. So many more of them around the town now. Holes in walls, holes in limbs, holes in habits, the hole in my stomach, the hole I dug.

I had a giddy thought.

I said to the teacher, 'I want to present a fake documentary on a detective story about holes. I call it *What's in a Hole?*'

The teacher bowed his head and listened. I suppose he felt he had to.

I stayed in the hole and pretended to hold a microphone, spoke at the wall because keeping my eyes on the teacher would give me a crick in the neck. I'd be the expert on holes after this. I began:

'Good evening, ladies and gentlemen, from a very tense region after a very difficult couple of days. The last troops have disappeared down the road, that road winding off to my rear.'

Distant explosions.

'To get a local perspective on what's happened here – let me step over this body – let's talk to one couple who would prefer to remain anonymous. Mr and Mrs Professor, as we shall call them, are about to take evening tea after a recent battle for their town.'

I hear Mr Professor's footsteps descending the stairs. This is exciting, of course, because a discussion of the philosophy of holes is sure to follow.

Mr Professor, who wears a moustache, comes back from the bathroom, says to Mrs Professor, 'Toilet is slow again.'

'Try getting a plumber now,' Mrs Professor says.

He points to the camera team and asks her, 'Who are these people?'

Mrs Professor opens her mouth to speak. But I have the microphone.

'We are the news. Sir, would you mind standing closer to the camera? We hear that you are unofficially called the Professor of Holes.'

'I am.' Fixing his glasses.

'You study the philosophy of holes.'

'I do.'

'Which is considered philosophically difficult.'

'It is.'

'Have you kept notes or written a book?'

'What is this? Who are you again?'

'We are filming a documentary on the origin and prevalence of holes.'

'With all this shooting going on?'

'It was scheduled for this week. We could of course look elsewhere for this documentary to be shown on *national television*.'

His startled look all of a sudden. 'Oh. Well, perhaps we can discuss this further. I'll have some tea and we can start. How is your tea?'

'Yes, we have information that you may have information about underground activity by an over-zealous student of philosophy who is rumoured to have discovered a way of accessing a different universe through drainpipes.'

'No.'

'You have been seen leaving the house after midnight with a flashlight, a notebook, and a heavy gabardine-style trench coat, a tweed hat, and what appears to be a pipe.'

'Good God man! You were having me watched!'

'We were having you researched.'

The professor looks at the camera and waves the sound down. I nod to the cameraman. The professor leans over to me and hides his mouth with a hand.

He says, 'I did hear about a strange student snooping around for clues on the nature of holes. Threatened a local university professor with a gun unless he gave her the main points of philosophical debate on the subject. Then left in search of the true nature of holes, what was really in them.'

(Of course, I motion the volume up while he's talking. People have a right to know. Mrs Professor pours tea. Close-up shot.)

He says, 'What did this student find? And did his search reveal anything about the disappearance of Flight 109? The lost civilization of Atlantis? The startling appearance of UFOs a mile wide over populated areas, hundreds of witnesses, film evidence, tracked by military radar, then disappearing without trace? One of the greatest secrets in popular science today is that people are very close to finding out the truth, and when they do, they will not survive it. But we, as news people, have an obligation to reveal what may be one of the deepest mysteries since the evidence of a burial place for Jesus in Kashmir. THEY ALL FELL INTO HOLES.'

Professor Hole, as we will call him for the documentary, whose face and voice will be altered for his safety, leads me out of the house and turns left after checking both sides of the street. Rubble everywhere. A sheet of rain. He lights his pipe and hikes his trench-coat collar around his neck and walks into the wind, the soles of his leather shoes clicking on the concrete.

I catch up, the microphone hoisted up to his face.

'Your impressions at this point?'

'The thing is,' he says, 'that many people believe that holes don't exist. That holes are part of a seeing process and have no existence outside the mind.'

'And your position? I mean, that sounds a little too convenient, doesn't it?'

'Not now. Here. We are nearing the clock.'

We stumble silently.

'Look at that clock,' he says.

'Point the camera,' I say to the cameraman.

The professor says, 'Does each passing second leave a hole behind it made of the second that has passed or is it replaced by the next second without any void created? Where does the second go? Where does it go? If we leave aside the notion of time, what could replace it? We get older. The grass grows. All these are processes. We have created a measurement to make them easy to talk about.'

'And what's in a hole, then?' I ask.

The professor rubs his chin. Clear that he knows the answer, obvious that he edits his response:

'What's in a hole can be *What did so-and-so do with his life?* He is in that hole. *What did I do last month?* That question is in the hole. *Where did the time go when I was young and carefree?* If I look into that type of hole, I'll find all my youth.'

'I see,' I say. 'And will you find yourself? Younger versions, perhaps? Lost friends? Experiences? First time you fell in love? What you felt when you saw a dead person?'

'I haven't figured that out yet,' he says thoughtfully, followed by a smile and a wink. I think he knows more than he tells me. Or is prepared to tell me.

'Einstein,' he says, 'knew that time was matter. That time and space could be warped and bent, like the dip in a stretched sheet if you place a stone in the middle. Ever notice how everything slows down when you go over the handlebars of your bike?'

'I have no bike, but, Professor, some people believe that since no holes exist, neither does the past.'

'Yes, and you can therefore deny that the past actually took place as it did, and rather insist that it happened only as you remember it. A very common occurrence these days.'

'Yes.'

'That nevertheless does not disprove that the past happened as you didn't *want* it to happen.'

'Ah, yes.' I scratch my head and then ask what I hope is not as cynical sounding as I want it to be: 'And the connection to holes?'

'Quiet a moment.' His hand over the lens. Satisfied, he steps onto the main street.

We pass under the town clock.

'The first thing you learn about this investigation is that there are different types of holes.'

'So you admit that holes exist,' I whisper.

He grabs my collar. Steel-grey eyes like nails.

'Yes, Mr Professor?'

'See that clock?'

'Yes.'

'See the hands, the minute hand?'

'Yes.'

'What's happening?'

'Nothing. They bombed it.'

'So is it a clock now?'

'Ah,' I say.

'You believe you see a clock, right?'

'Yes.'

'That doesn't mean it exists.'

'But I can see it. It's right there.'

Mr Professor says, 'Holes present the same problem for those who study knowledge. Do holes exist? What is a hole?'

Suddenly his hand pulls my head down and he turns to face the wall. An army truck roars by.

'Sorry about that. We can't be seen here.' He sighs. 'A hole is how water spills out of the bucket, right? How you lose the coins in your pocket.'

'Yes.'

'Wrong.'

He really sounds like a detective. I try to mumble this into the microphone as, stumbling over the rubble, we reach an open space. He pulls me to the wall of a pineapple-pocked office building. Through the gaps in the frontage, people on the street, even now, shadowy figures in the smoke, hard to tell if they are combatants or fleeing citizens.

'It's like this,' the professor says, looking at the camera.

I'm saying, 'No, look at me.'

'It's like this. A student at the local university found out that holes may not exist. Got it from a book, of course, the last place you want to learn anything from. A little learning, you know.'

I nod, 'Of course, Professor.'

'This student got wind of the fact that there are two and only two options for understanding holes. That's why the student held up the faculty member in the philosophy of science and demanded his complete notes. A gun brandished, I hear. Empty chambers, probably. Left with a sheaf of papers and that's all I know.'

'So he could be anywhere,' I say.

'She.'

'Of course. Could be anywhere. Professor, you were leading me to the next item you uncovered in your investigation.'

His hand sweeps across the open space, once a park.

'Yes?' I ask.

'I have nothing to say about the park. I was stretching my arm muscles.'

He turns to the wall. The secret theory of holes. 'Look at this wall, the bullet and shell holes. Are they holes?' he asks.

I place my fingers in the holes.

'Yes,' I say, 'these are holes. No doubt about it.'

'Keep your fingers where they are. Listen carefully. Some would say that the wall here is torn or parts of it are missing, but there is no hole. If more of the wall gets blown away, less material creates the illusion we call a hole. A doughnut is ringed, it doesn't have a hole. A circular amount of doughnut material is missing.'

'Hmmm.'

'But that's not the fascinating part.' Mr Professor leans closer, collar up, eyes darting furtively around as we huddle to the wall. 'Holes may exist anyway.'

He continues, 'Holes may exist, but we see them as part of the objects surrounding them. The problem is, what would you have to do to make a hole bigger? How could you be inside a hole? You are instead inside the space from the missing material of the surrounding object. How can coins fall through a hole? The coins are held in place by the pocket

lining, they take up a certain volume and fall at a
certain speed. That's what you see. The hole is just a
concept. You have to be careful, very careful.'

'We have six minutes of tape left, Mr Professor.'

'Apparently this student found some evidence that
a philosopher called John Locke, long dead, suggested
that holes are not things and therefore cannot cause
anything to happen. Thus seeing a hole is part of an
illusion. You misspell a word but it still looks like the
word to your eye because that's what it expects to see.
Holes get away with it.'

He leans closer, 'They get away with murder.
Holes cover it up.'

'Four minutes, Professor. What have you discovered
about holes?'

Mr Professor digs his hands deep into his pockets
and snarls.

'Patience. Let me finish the philosophical
groundwork first. According to the academy, holes
may be missing parts of objects. Yet in the final
analysis, holes may be simply holes. If so, they are
parasites. You can't separate the hole from the
material. Holes are space but not like real space. You
can fill them, fall into them, measure them.'

'Can you break a hole?' I ask.

'Ha!' he says. 'Brilliant question! You can't have
bits of a hole, so the answer must be a "no" on that.
Now, follow me.'

I follow the professor in his swirling coat through
the acrid smell of carbonate. The silence after battle.
Smoke like weeds growing from cracks and craters.

We reach a hole in which a soldier lies crumpled, his face shot through. Professor gestures for the camera. 'We put our dead in holes,' he says. 'Then we ritually destroy the hole by filling it in. They'll carry him to another hole and bury him. Is it still a hole?'

'Definitely a thought to ponder,' I say.

Tank tracks clanking. A shot, two shots, a series of gun bursts.

'A counterattack, some guerillas maybe,' says the professor. 'We must leave now. We'll be shot if we're found near this man.'

We run back to the professor's house. I note how cleanly he moves for a man his age. Near the house, we both gasp as we see soldiers running from the front door, guns blazing, a man falling. Obviously, the professor is anguished.

'My wife!' the professor shouts and speeds up.

We race back, ladies and gentlemen. Entering the house. And as we might suspect, Mrs Professor is gone. On a hunch I run to the drainpipe. A left shoe and a pair of glasses abandoned at the spewing end. She used the exit to another dimension. But surely that's too small a hole, the drainpipe, to get into such a big hole, another dimension?

My conclusion: more questions, ladies and gentlemen, can it be that Mrs Professor is the real detective? She played us. Is she the real student who held up the faculty member? An accomplice? More missing parts in the ancient mystery of holes?

A murky end to what may be a long chase.

Mr Professor is inside, pretending to search frantically for his wife.

Let's question Mr Professor, on whether he is indeed the ranking authority on holes in this house. But first, a few final words.

Einstein in 1905 maintained that time and space change at close to light speed: distance stretches, time passes more slowly than normal time. Black holes are an example of gravity from which nothing, including light, can escape. When gravity is too strong to support even itself, it collapses in on itself and drags after it every atom of matter within a huge radius, like Cygnus X-1, a black hole thirty times bigger than the sun. Inside? Other universes, stacked one inside the other, like Russian dolls? A different kind of matter?

Holes are dangerous things, best left for the experts to fill in. But the question remains, What is *in* a hole?

This I intend now to ask the professor. I see a fleeting shape dash past me.

'Who's that running?' I say. 'Wait, what's this? Professor! Professor! Why are you running away? Professor, what do you have to hide? [*Panting*] Our viewers have a right to know! The world does! We'll show your face if you don't talk to us! What's that in the sky? Hey, point the camera at the sky! There, there! Did you get that? It shot out of the drainpipe. Some sort of projectile. Yes, out of the drainpipe! Didn't you get it? Oh, Jesus tap-dancing Christ, I screamed at you to point the camera at the sky!

'I saw Mrs Professor, I saw her at the helm of the projectile. I saw the man's wife, I tell you. Don't shake your head at me!'

———

I catch my breath. The wind lightens and snow falls gently into the hole.

'Is the documentary still running?' asked the teacher.

'No, it's over.'

'I wasn't shaking my head at you,' he said.

'I got carried away. I'm hungry. That happens, you know.'

He smiled, 'I know.' He straightened his coat and stretched, made little jumps and some waist twisting. Nice for him up there in the wide-open field.

I said aloud, 'Black holes, I'm not afraid of them at all. Whirling powerhouses in space.'

The teacher said, 'That's what claustrophobia feels like. A life lived badly. Trapped in elevator, under sheets, too many people on the footpath. I want to be at home, in the garden, in a fresh breeze by the sea with nothing before my eyes but water. Sometimes my very breath gets trapped in me, everything constricts. I fall to a thousandth of my size, gravity has nowhere to go, so it stabs a hole into another universe and claws its way out like a trapped rat through a burning shed wall. I have a dread of being confined in a small space. What's inside a black hole? It's like asking, What's inside of death? If you don't like the rules of the game, step out of the machine and turn it off. You like black holes, Baker? Bars, movie theatres, cocaine, fast cars, dreaming. People live in them who have turned off the entire universe, let the lights go out for ever on their hopes.'

I said, 'In that case, a black hole is what I'm standing in.'

The Sun Won't Wait

The teacher must have regretted his outburst about black holes. Maybe he wanted me to open up, follow his little lead, his obvious encouragement. Something about last-minute confessions seems so desperate. I mean, people have their whole lives to say these things if they must.

He lit a double-digit cigarette and almost drank in the nicotine. Although the afternoon had sunk below the horizon, his face gleamed like a pale plate or the moon on a blue afternoon. Something was up with him.

I paced the hole, now a few minutes from total dark, and thought how I hadn't seen the sun go down.

I kicked a foothold in the wall and hitched myself up on it to see what was happening. More activity by the wall. The six lines shuffled forward a few metres, then stopped at a whistle thinly piercing the wind gusts and blasts of snow. I guessed that it was well past three o'clock now, the deadline for the hole to be finished. And I was at least thirty minutes away from finishing.

He said, 'I have something to tell you.'

I turned.

PIECES

What was he about to say, and why did he stop?

He cupped a hand over his eyes and peered across the field. I jumped as high as I could and glimpsed a shadow in the snow swirls.

I jumped again. The shadow a boy, no more than eleven or twelve years old. Running, stumbling.

I jumped again.

'It's one of my students,' the teacher said. 'I recognize the cap.'

I waited in the hole as the boy reached our position.

'Please help me. I am looking for my parents, my family!'

I stayed low in the hole, preferring by first instinct to let the teacher get rid of him. It was hard to hear everything, so I kicked another foothold in the clay and climbed up the side of the hole and listened with a hand to my ear. The teacher first calmed the boy down and asked him questions.

'And what happened then?' the teacher asked.

'The trees took my parents. They walked into the trees at the edge of the village with the soldiers and I have not seen them since. In that field there – no, that one – I saw a long hole dug. My grandmamma used to joke that if I was a bad boy, the ghosts would come to get me. I think they came and got her.'

'And what happened then?'

'The villagers decided to stay even though they knew the soldiers were coming. The soldiers came into each of the houses along our street. I heard gunshots. We were the last house in our row. I ran to the window and saw them leave our neighbour's house and turn for ours. I shouted to my family, "Now it is our turn," but everyone just sat still. One of the soldiers entered our house and sat at our table and lit a cigarette. He asked my uncle to leave. The soldier said, "Why will you not leave? You have no choice," and he raised his gun. Then my uncle grabbed his eye and called out. My cousin held his stomach and opened his mouth. He fell and broke like a glass on the floor, like when I dropped mother's family vase when I was five – no, five and a half – and she cried because it was her own mother who gave it to her, but she held me anyway and said it was okay. I've told you already that the trees took my mother and father.'

'And what happened then, with the soldiers?'

'The soldier did not shoot me. He left with the others and walked to a field. They were strong, naked from the waist up. Their muscles were big. They wore sunglasses and scarves around their heads. I told my uncle and cousin I would come back, and I followed the soldiers through the trees. They walked to a field and sat down with their rifles in the wildflowers. I walked out of the trees and one of them pointed his rifle at me, but I said quickly, my heart beating so fast, that I wanted to make them tea, I would find everything I needed to make the tea, and ask them to bring my parents back if I was nice to them. I would follow them and make them tea. They laughed. One said, "We'll be back to kill you."

'I said, "I will polish your boots too. Will you bring them back now?" They said my sister was in a car. I looked behind them and saw a hand in the grass.'

'And what happened then?'

'I ran to tell Grandmamma. I recognized her house, which was burning, by the curtains. I went upstairs to Grandmamma, holding a sock in front of my mouth because of the smoke. She sat in her bedroom and I think I heard her say my name. Her hand always shook when she held out fresh biscuits to me when I was younger, but now her hand reached out to me still and steady. Her eyes, always wet, were dry and clear now. Her voice was not the strong voice that called to me when I was much younger, when I made my first steps. I heard gunfire outside. I crawled to where she was sitting and said, "I am a man now, Grandmamma, let me cook for you," but she shook her head. "Let me, let me," I said to her. She shook her head again and again. She did not move from the armchair. I shook her shoulder, and her head shook again. Her skin was cold. Her clear eye watched me without blinking. She was holding her breath. After telling my grandmamma I would be back, I ran outside, along the walls where I played before the soldiers came. The walls where I played had bullets in them. And the houses on the other side of the street had turned to shells.

'When the soldiers bombed the street, I ran to the village square and dug a hole in the pile of timber and stone and waited a long time after the explosions had stopped. But I got hungry and looked over the edge of the hole, saw nothing, and walked to the edge of the village, where the main road runs past. I saw lines of people from other towns hurry along the road. I looked for something to eat. All that day the same people who had run in one direction returned, staring. Their eyes were bigger because they had seen a lot of things that had to be kept in them. They pushed prams and tractors filled with their goods. The ground shook, made my bones shake. I slept when I was tired.'

'And what happened then?'

'I went to the field where the soldiers had gone after shooting my uncle and cousin. The soldiers had gathered there again to rest, the rifles used on my uncle and cousin beside them. I looked behind the soldiers and saw bones in a suit of clothes on the grass.

'I asked the soldiers, "Who will love me?" They said, "Ask your mother." And they laughed. I told them that they should not say things like that. They did not shoot me. I went back to my village. The sky was empty all along one side because the houses were gone now, and my grand-mamma's house was gone with them. The crows were gone because the trees were gone. I ran for another day until my feet bled first and then got sore. I ran until I caught up with the other villagers who had hurried through our village on the way to the mountains. They said they could not feed me. They sent me back.'

'What happened then?'

'I found food and stole more from soldiers who remained to guard the village. It got cold and I got careless. But they caught me stealing yesterday and fired at me. I ran and ran until they stopped shooting and when I looked back I could-n't see them any more. Then I ran all night and now I saw you standing in the field. Then you asked me questions.'

I saw the teacher lean down to the boy and take his hand, but the boy shook it clear.

'I am not a little boy!'

'No, you are grown now, a man.'

'Can you help me find my family? I want my mamma and papa! I want my sister! I am alone! I am hungry!'

The teacher opened his eyes wide and shouted, 'Leave here now. Run, run! Go!'

'No, I want to stay with you.'

'You'll do nothing like that. Here, be off with you!'

I saw the teacher's hand rise as if to strike him or throw a rock.

The boy's cap bobbed across the hole's rim and I watched as the teacher's head followed it. I jumped and saw the boy struggling away from us through the snow and to the forest. The teacher watched him for a long minute, and when he turned again and faced me, I knew that his student, along with his hunger and his hopeless search, had gone.

PART III

4:00 p.m.

DAVID HUME AND THE
BLACK DOG

'What time is it?' I asked.

'Close to four.' The answer mechanical.

'And the deadline?'

'Are you in a hurry?' he asked.

'No.'

The teacher went silent, his eyes glazed with a smearing of thought. Then he stood at the edge, watched me carefully and said, 'David Hume, the philosopher and psychologist, you know of him by any chance?'

'Of course I do,' I said. *Never heard of him.*

'Then you may know that he suffered a type of nervous occurrence as a youth, a complete deadening of his sensibilities, which may explain why he argued later that a person's identity is unstable. In my mind the two events are linked. That collapse had a huge effect on him.' And he curled his palm into a fist.

'Baker, it was the black dog, you see.'

I didn't know whether the teacher was baiting me because I had perhaps revealed too much of myself to him when I said I was standing in a black hole.

'What happened to him?' I asked. 'What dog?'

'He wrote a letter,' the teacher said.

'Yes?'

'In 1734 he wrote a letter to Dr George Cheyne. I remember it because I've often read it to my students, many of whom, especially young men, find themselves overcome by the simple act of being alive.'

'The letter?' I said.

'Hume told Cheyne that, at the beginning of September 1729, his ardour for life and books and thinking extinguished themselves in a passing moment. And that since then, he could no longer lift his thinking to that pitch that once gave him pleasure. A coldness, he described it. A desertion. And it remained for nine months, no better, no worse. The doctors, useless. So he studied the philosophy of truth and reflected on death.'

'What? He had a cold?' I asked. 'A virus?'

'A deeper fatigue, Baker. The black dog. It comes to young and old, all races, all places, and it lies upon their head and casts a shadow on every feeling, presses a weight on every thought. Scratches out a circle and sleeps dully inside the glass of their soul. Men have called it by different names for thousands of years.'

'Look, I can't stand around here all day. What exactly happened to Hume?'

'Beyond his letter, I don't know. You see, Hume wrote that seven months later, a doctor gave Hume some anti-hysteric pills, put him on a course of bitters. Hume also drank a pint of claret wine and rode eight or ten miles every day. Although he couldn't quite get back to the higher flights of his spirits, he felt better. He made himself work less, eat sensibly. He continued for seven months in this manner. Uneasily.'

'Why? You said Hume was better. He said he was better.'

'Because the dog was still at the door, wagging its tail,

tongue out for some attention. And it got in the door again when Hume wasn't looking. In April 1741 Hume went from being tall and lean to fat and with heart palpitations in six weeks. His friends congratulated him on his stout appearance and recovery. His family thought him in good humour and a better companion than ever before. He took hope from their observations despite his inner feeling and rode eight miles twice a day, renewed the bitters and pills and visited a famous mineral well. But the dog was upon him. He perceived through desperate study a strong connection between mind and body.'

'Aimless wandering of the mind,' I said, more to keep the teacher from the stage than to offer an opinion. He was drawing such a huge map for me. No wonder my brother learned nothing from this man. All talk and no learning. No point.

I flung down the shovel and sighed.

The teacher did not flinch, said, 'He studied the moral philosophy of the ancients and faulted them for inventing schemes of living that depended, as he said, more on invention than human experience. You see, Hume believed all moral conclusions should be based on human nature. He looked at his former writing and saw only what he called "pages and pages of my own invention", fancy, make-believe.'

The teacher closed a fist. 'And then Hume's next problem surfaced. The one that made him suffer.'

'What now?' I said.

'He couldn't concentrate on the details any more, couldn't make all those details into fine, elegant prose, all the parts of his thinking, in fluid lines. Looked away every ten minutes. He couldn't concentrate enough to write his ideas.'

I said, 'I am getting fed up, and this is just pure cruelty on your part. I don't have to take any of this, this rambling.'

At once, the teacher's hands went up in a wave. 'No, no. I have a point. Please be patient. Please hear me out.'

I stared and he took this as a Yes.

He said, 'Hume couldn't ignore the tiny interval of mental movement between his state and perfect health, since he had no outward appearance of illness. That distance tormented him. And he imagined the distance between his "distemper and vapours," as they called things then, and madness, as being just as small. Maybe he could slide further. He finished the letter by saying that he had not come out of the cloud, that he despaired of ever recovering. *Whether I can hope for a Recovery? Whether I must long wait for it? Whether my Recovery will ever be perfect, and my Spirits regain their former Spring and Vigour? Whether I have taken a right way to recover? I believe all proper medicines have been used, and therefore need mention nothing of them.* So sad, Baker.'

I rubbed my forehead with a cold glove, 'So you don't know what happened then?'

'No. I honestly do not know, and I never bothered to find out. You see, the beauty of the letter is the enquiry, the humaneness, the honesty, the fear and bewilderment. Despite all his learning, Hume knew he was in trouble.'

I said, 'And all of this has been for what use? There's a storm blowing and time is passing, remember?'

'What do you conclude from Hume's symptoms?' the teacher said.

'I conclude, Teacher, that they don't write letters like that any more. It's called a telephone,' I said dryly. *Good to get a gut punch in at this point.* Smelled his own salts a little too much, a bit of a mirror lover, this man of letters.

'The black dog, Baker, is depression. The spirit siphoned away. The dog robs people of their vital life like a thief a handbag on a crowded street. And you look around and say, *where did it go?* You stand in a fog and can't touch the real world. You look much the same as you did before, you sound the same. But you are a ghost. Absent from your own life. An inch to the side, one step away from happiness.'

'I have heard of depression.' My heart raced. The teacher had just described my life.

The teacher said, 'I'm sure you have.'

'What do you mean?'

'Maybe you have it.'

I laughed because that's all I could do. No thoughts formed in my head that I could throw back at him. I was watching a man coming apart with rage or some passion, a man hitting the truth with every swing.

'I'm the same man I've always been,' I said.

'You must have it. How else could you have done the things you've done? How could you have lost your revulsion so easily? Maybe you feel the same as Hume, maybe this helps you recognize. I want you to see, Baker. All this can't be in vain. What have you—'

'No—'

'—discovered?'

'I'm not in the least bit sad.'

'No! It's not sadness!' he shouted. 'It's black bile. The black dog. So many names, so many lives, so many thousands of years. For heaven's sake, even a few pills might have restored you.'

'I'm not sad. Maybe you should try those pills, Teacher.'

He said, 'Maybe the black dog found you one day in your bakery. Crept up on you. Maybe that's the detachment in you. Maybe that's why you did it.' And he pointed down into the hole at me, 'I want to know!'

I said, 'Listen to you. You're the one who's depressed. Haven't you got anything else to think about but failures, Hume and all those other failures?'

And we faced off, and only driving snow filled the space between us.

A COLLABORATOR SPEAKS

This part of the country is a peninsula. The main coastal town is only a few miles away. Boardwalks fly flags for each townland, some ferries dock there in summer, though we're too far north for the sunseekers, though a good summer surprised us four years ago with six weeks of never-ending days. The young girls dressed scantily, and the young boys wore shorts and white shirts. Everyone went to the beaches, and the talk of war and the constant threats of war evaporated. This is glove-and-scarf country for most of the year. And for most of the year, we wear those gloves and scarves and we keep our heads down and we mind our own business.

Sometimes, however, people may decide that they want to mind your business. And it's a lucky man who can resist them, especially if they have the weapons.

I could not resist.

The dark heaved its dirt on me in the hole, and I felt the urge to talk.

'Teacher,' I shouted.

No response.

'Hey, I'm in here! I want to talk!'

He appeared, a line of snow across his shoulders and head as if he'd been highlighted with paste. His face a mix of blue, ink, and white frost on his eyelids.

'Teacher, do you still want to know?'

He folded his arms. At that moment, though I could not be sure, I felt the last of the light finally lift away and fly off past the trees. We were in the second half of the afternoon or the first half of night. The world was turning and we with it.

'The soldiers came to my house,' I said.

'We knew that. We were watching.'

'They came to my house the evening of that first day, came from the beer hall and gave me a minute to decide if I wanted life or death. I was an able-bodied man, single, and strong from years of carrying baskets of bread. In my situation, one could normally expect to be worked to death or shot.'

'I understand.'

'If I helped them, acted as a policeman of my own people, did some odd jobs, I would outlive the conflict. Of course I agreed.'

'Of course,' he replied, pursing his lips around the cigarette. 'You were lucky. I myself might have agreed,' he crushed the butt, 'if they'd asked me.'

'They didn't,' I said.

'And here we are,' he said.

'No, not quite. Here I am and there you are.'

'I feel worse about this, because you're one of us,' he said. I saw his mouth shake and wondered what he wanted from me.

I asked, 'Do you want me to say I'm sorry? Is that what you want to hear?'

He withdrew into the howling.

Types of Wind and
Their Effect on the
Human Condition

I have read in detail about the effects of wind on the human condition. In those books, I think the writers were philosophers of wind. You see – and I'll use their kinds of words – in windy, northland country you'll hear many different words in the directories of human reference for wind: whisper, breeze, gust, blast. The word that describes a barely detectible tremor on a spring pond, the word for the draught that brings a mile-deep ocean to roiling heights. Movement of air across a flat or undulating landscape, a city or traceless chalk without a footprint. Wind, the geographer says, can be warm, cold, ice-bludgeoning, straight-line, or, in the present case, a blustery gale that bears snow, a type of blizzard, except that you can see for a hundred metres in any direction, if you can bring yourself to look. Wind here blows down from the hardy scrubs of the north tundra. It beats down the stable objects that grow in its path, bushes, small saplings bent before the prevailing wind. Less stable objects like humans habitually fork even on windless days, since they press into the wind rather than away from it, so that when a day is calm they saunter gaily in mild surprise as if relieved of a debt or a bad arrangement of some kind. Even less stable objects like water – well, let me tell you, the main town in this province fronts the coast, a blue expanse on good days, a vast slate in overcast conditions, little foam flags under black cloud if the wind is west off the sea. On this bleak day the town and its hinterland lay a few inches under fine cold wet broken frozen pieces of white rain harried like worried sheep into swirls and bunches ahead of the wind. Wind is another word for weather. This weather here in this place heaps a slap into your face. You can debate the climate, but sooner or later you'll have to step into it. It hits you. To hell with the philosophy of wind. When I cough it's wind, talk it's wind, snore it's wind. Wind is a rumour of another baker who sets up in town, wind is what's between coins in my till, wind is what gets into your brain and turns you soft if you let goodness and kindness fill the days of your life, or whatever the saying is. Make wind move and you'll be all right. Let it sit in you and you'll burst. Lift a cheek, don't turn a cheek. The weather had it in for me since I was a child. Got soaked on the way to the school, sat for hours in wet clothes. As an adult, wet on the way to the bakery, worked in a wet shirt. The wind and its cousin the rain became my enemies. That's my philosophy of wind.

How the Baker
Constructed His Oven

Probably past four o'clock.

To hell with it, I couldn't see anything. Stab my foot if I kept at it. Enough. The end. I had finished the hole. Who would measure it anyway? I left the shovel and the pickaxe in one corner and walked up and down, flapped my arms. I counted ten steps long, four wide.

I wanted to talk to myself. Explain something to myself.

One day I dug a hole in my garden.

After work, one evening about two weeks ago, an envelope arrived, a pamphlet I had ordered on how to construct a brick oven. If you want to be exact, a retained heat masonry oven. And how important that moment was in my life, for I had never actually built anything before. That's why I'm being so exact, why I'm using a lot of words, because I want no misunderstandings.

In the bathroom I closed the window and shut out the dark bare November trees and sat on the toilet. There it was! The instruction, the diagrams, the illustrations, the time frame. Two days! A small, simple, wood-powered, dry-clay brick oven. I devoured the pages; my eyes burned into a slit.

This is how I did it.

First Step. I dug a hole in my garden, made a concrete pad, mixed concrete and poured it as a block base and for the hearth.

Second Step. I marked out the centre lines and laid out the hearth. I had chosen 2 by 3 metres as the size.

Third Step. I set the hearth with firebricks above a mortar bed of fireclay and sand, putting dry joints between the firebricks. I positioned the bricks correctly with a deadblow mallet. Then I used the spirit level to even the lines and finally just stood back and used ordinary unaided eyesight to check the lines. I did not let any tree lines or house lines throw me off.

Fourth Step. I built up the sidewalls and marked the mortar joints; then I built the back gable walls and washed the bricks.

Fifth Step. I created the layout for the arch on wood, using a string to calculate the right angle of arc so that I could use all whole bricks instead of having to spilt them (tedious and time-consuming). I measured a height of 40 cm above the hearth.

Sixth Step. I cut the arc out of the wooden board with a saw and nailed the structure together; then I built up the front apron using clay bricks and mortar.

That was the first day.

On the second day I laid the vault, with the wooden arch structure supporting each ring of bricks. As each ring hardened and set, I moved the arch forward after I'd filled in the mortar joints. Then the hardest part: I narrowed the vault down to the door opening and constructed the vault corners. Then I put mesh over the vault and plywood for the padding.

End of the second day.

On the third day I chopped wood in the forest and stored it in my shed. The pamphlet estimated that 80 kg of wood would fire the oven for 800 hours at the correct temperature.

And on the fourth day I lit the wood under the hearth and baked my flatbreads and consumed them with a cold beer, because I sweat easily, even though it was a cold day. My garden was small, my house small, my oven small, small bread, small stomach, small is the taste of bread. Small is the taste of bread, *oh bread, bread,* let it swim on your tongue and make taste to you, wheat paste and firewood. Master of my dominion, king with a castle in town and a weekend estate. A bakery in all places, a retreat, should the castle ever be stormed! Sweet bread, sweet fire, musty wood in my arms, wood tumbling falling into the sub-hearth, fire destroying bark, hard wood, ash, beech, oak, all types, into the fire, into the fire with you and from that heat comes the sweetest bread, the freshest taste in the world. The taste of bread. Bread. Jesus lives in it these days. Even he lives in it.

Bread! Bread! Bread! Bread! Bread! And Bread!

A neighbour's fat cat watched me with one eye. I threw a stone.

Spy.

Are You Ready for Your Trial?

'Are you ready for your trial?' The teacher's coat draped from him, his shoulders hunched, his legs together, his arms folded.

'What trial and what are you talking about and are you an idiot?' I shouted this as fast as I could.

'Do you want a representative?'

'No. What? No!' I didn't want misunderstandings. If the teacher was going mad, I needed to calm him down.

'Do you have a wife we don't know about? Children? Are your parents alive?'

'I cannot talk about my parents.'

'Wife?'

'I do not have a wife, never needed one.'

He said, 'You have to be represented.'

'I represent myself.'

And he stepped back again, and the wind covered the top of the hole with a sheen of sleet, like clear plastic drawn across it.

I thought desperately. It would be dangerous to climb out of the hole in the dark. Stay in here. Delay the teacher. *Delay him.*

The Baker's Theories
on Women

I would talk to delay him. What to talk about, though? Wife. Women. A man like him, cultured and all that, has a woman, of course. But what to talk about, if we talk about women?

Can men live without women? I thought. Good discussion. Make him feel he's in class again, doing his preaching. Subject under discussion: Are men harder or softer without women? Are they happier without women? Without women. Without women. Women without men without women. I spoke to the teacher:

'I need to discuss something with you that comes under the realm of philosophy and such things.'

'Yes?' He didn't look all that interested. I think he was finished with me. I didn't want that. Too much could go wrong.

'Men without women in the world,' I said. 'Wouldn't that just drag us all back to the ABCs? Back to how to read a new language of life, I suppose.'

'Is this you talking now?' the teacher asked me.

'Of course. Can't you hear me? Do I not speak these words out of my own mouth?'

'You say a lot of things, but mostly it's what you glean from books.'

'This is my theory on women. Mine and mine alone, yes, assembled from books, I'll admit that; but I assembled it myself!'

But I would say what the teacher wanted to hear.

'Very well,' he said.

I said, 'Women get to you, don't they? I mean to you, Teacher. But you were born alone and you'll die alone, woman or no woman, that's what I say.'

I continued, speaking faster, my head filled with words that followed one another, and I hoped they'd make sense of me.

I said, 'I've read about the whole phenomenon. Look, marriage is only about a thousand years old as we know it. Church found a way of licensing it for filthy lucre. That was it. You want to be married? Okay, here's the guild's stamp of approval. That'll be fifty notes, mate. Flocks of sheep to it, of course. Halleluiah and organ music, rice, promises to keep, white meaning I'm fresh, you can write all over me. Men without women? No, it's back to the ABCs, if you had to learn life all over again with no women anywhere on the planet.'

'How would we—'

'Propagation? Reproduction through what you say, the right sequence of words.'

'For the love of Jesus.'

'Women have never existed in this plan, this vision, so don't for-the-love-of-Jesus me, Teacher. I've worked the whole thing out. Weeks, it took me.'

He stared at me as I spoke too fast to draw a proper breath.

'Now, as I was saying, the right sequence of words. Something like, Hello, how are you doing? That will bear a girl (sorry, no girls). Nice weather, what are your plans today? That's a boy embryo. So you really have to be careful who you talk to. Simple conversation and suddenly you're a father. Men everywhere. Men and boys and old men and men in their forties. Men in windows. Men in the park. Men in the fields. Men at home. Men at work. Men playing games. Men at concerts. Men eating in restaurants. Sex not an issue, sex not even a thought.'

The teacher said, 'You are insane.'

'Watch your words, Teacher. I am not as powerless as you think. I still have influence. Now, as I was saying, on the subject of war: men fight naturally, and this will of course continue in my visionary world, but not over women. Oh no! No face launching a million ships, as I read once. They'll fight over what they really need, and no man really needs a woman. He *thinks* he does. So I proclaim the new alphabet for a man's world!'

'I am listening.'

'I present my new alphabet! A is for the apple that I never ate. B is for battle and what I can win. C is for cunt because I know you were thinking that as I said it. D is for development of biceps, and E is for even if I don't masturbate I don't have to think about it because penises are for pissing. F is for Hello, what are your plans for today?'

'You are insane. Admit everything now, your collaboration, and be done with it.'

'G is for glancing over the pink stratums of man's flesh covering the entire globe with skin. H is for the entire and enormous and very significant word "Hard" or its opposite, "Hardly." I is for the world as it should be, and J is for Juniper, the final ingredient in mountain soup for survivors (and by the way, J is really another I, added recently by Mr Johnson in his dictionary).'

'I believe you.'

'K is for calamity with a capital K. L is for letters or titles, as in Lieutenant-General Captain Blitzkrieg III, and M performs the same function, as in Major-General Corporal someone. N is for nice when I'm not fighting you; O is for opus, all music, all literature. P is for passion, for all the ways the letters of the alphabet can mingle to make a new word that means something to come, as in a mystical awareness, a power to excite. Q is for quiet, at night, early, at dawn's touch, when the ceiling lowers and looks at you quizzically. R is for being right.'

'You are never wrong.'

'S is not for sex, and T is for treachery, a woman's web we'll soon tear from the four corners of the world. U is for uterus, now piled in scrapyards; V is for vulva, similarly stacked but to the moon. W is for women, belonging at the end of the list because they have fallen off the world. X is for the roadblocks that capture the last of them, the stragglers, the ones who believe this isn't really happening. Y is for questions that come when I lie awake with the blanket clutched around my chin. Z is for sleep, what I can't get for a long time now.'

I was done. Now I wanted to hear his response. I had heard from my brother that the teacher, despite his shortcomings, often said interesting things. I wanted to hear what he had to say about women. The teacher left the edge of the hole and I shouted after him because he didn't need to go getting anyone yet.

'I'm not done with the hole!' I yelled. 'The snow keeps undoing my work. I'm not done!'

I grabbed the shovel and attacked the snow, sent wafts of

it above my head. I could still dig, the hole needed to be deeper, and I was the man to do it.

'Sissy Pus is still at work!' I roared above the wind.

He came back.

'Tantalus too.' He gazed at me.

'Tantalus?' I said.

'He offended the gods in Greek myth. They put him up to his neck in a river and dangled fruit above his head. Every time he reached for it, the fruit backed up precisely the same distance. Every time he tried to drink from the river, the water receded from his lips, just out of reach.'

'What did he do to deserve that?'

'Took something and wouldn't give it back. Something that belonged to the gods.'

I said, 'He took something that belonged to the gods? Talk about bringing a knife to a gunfight.'

'And King Midas, everything he touched turned to gold.'

'Rich but no bitch.'

'An astute observation, my loaf-making friend. Yes, all the wealth in the world but not an ounce of love. I'm too cold to laugh at what you've just said, Rich but no bitch, but I want to. You surprise me sometimes.'

He laughed anyway and said, 'I like that in you.'

I asked him, 'What do you believe about women? What do you, to use your favourite word, *understand* about them?'

This would buy me time if nothing else did. Information I could use, even if I could never employ it exactly. He chose not to answer me directly, as was his way. He cupped his hands over his mouth.

'Winter here cancels you out,' he said, grimacing into the wind. 'I mean it takes all of the experiences you've squeezed into memory and ejects them, shivers and shakes them completely through every pore in your body. Look at the town. Any town in a winter country. Induced by fear of being lonely and cold, men drift into bars and drink to push back the despair and pull forward the dreams of greatness that were their constant companions when young.'

I thought it funny that he shouted all this.

I answered, 'Now I asked you about women, and you talked philosophy and winter, but I want to know about women, your ideas, that is. I shared mine with you. It's only fair that you do the same for me, isn't that only fair?'

'You don't get it, Baker. You haven't been around many women, I can tell, so how can I explain anything to you that you'd understand?'

'Let's forget about understanding. I want to know everything: what you think of them.'

He said, 'Every word out of your mouth is a certainty or a desire for one. Your favourite words are *all*, *every*, *always*. Happiness, I've learned, lies in between those words, not in them. It took me forty years to learn that truth.'

'I'm still waiting for your ideas about women. I don't want to understand happiness or what my favourite words are.'

'My knowledge of women is one woman, a woman I've loved since I knew how to, without whom life would have little meaning, the trees no colour, the grass no song.'

'Whatever you say. She'll do, then.'

'She's not a subject for discussion.'

'But—'

'Not with you,' he looked to one side, 'or with anyone else.'

He wiped a hand across his forehead, rolled his shoulders, hand again, over his hair. Nervous obviously about something. I could tell he feared my question, so I pressed in for the attack.

'You don't really know anything about the ladies, do you? Just one. That's not enough for me. I'm sorry, I presumed you knew more than you do. I'm so sorry.'

He shook his head and sighed. Couldn't tell if he was patronizing me. First he just glared at me, then glanced around the hole as if deliberating whether to jump in or not, then shook a finger at me.

'You bait well, Baker.'

'What do women know?'

'I will guess what women know.'

'How?'

'By looking at you. You!'

'An insult, I'm sure, but I can listen to your proof.'

Down he came, in one jump, into the hole with me. I backed away.

The shovel and pickaxe were behind me, thank God.

PROOF THAT MEN EXIST

His coat brushed against me and I recoiled.

His mouth open like a cave.

'Proof? Proof? Proof that men like you exist is that wives at home press their faces into pillows and dream that a stranger who knows their bodies presses into them, into them deliciously, into them with a cock, any cock, any balls brushing their thighs, waves of pleasure, licking, stroking them up into tight, clenched joy that they hold on to as long as they can, and then they slide back to the bed or the pillow and their men who are nowhere to be found, even when they are in the same room. Men drift, women think. Men drift away and don't come back. They don't take the time to learn women's bodies. They want their pleasure fast and now, and then they want to sleep in the dark where another relief awaits them. And the women lie beside their sleeping men, touch themselves into a lonely ecstasy to finish the journey that their men start but can't bring to a close. Men start things they can't finish. They dirty their clothes and throw them in a pile. They conceive children and throw them in a pile. They say they love women but don't even like them. They want to travel the world but can't get past the television. They drift into old age and their blood turns bitter and disappointed. Other women become attractive to them because their wives have failed to keep themselves up. In cafés, you can see it. You're a wife talking to your husband, talking to him, and his eyes lift an inch above and beyond your shoulders. You look behind at a woman, young, pretty, who looks down quickly to a magazine she isn't reading, stifling a smile.

'Women aren't jealous of men,' the teacher said, 'they're jealous of the life men have failed to bring them. They lie beside their men in the night and are young and beautiful again. Their bellies shrink and their thighs firm. Men watch them and want them. They are no longer desperate. They no longer despair of being trapped in the fantasies they build to survive another day. They lie beside their men and hope that tomorrow will bring a new strength, a new face, a stranger's touch, a novel in the form of a perfect day, a different day from all the rest, that lifts their experiences from the page and undresses them seamlessly and breathlessly with its words, and says *Now you can live life. Live in these better days instead from now on*. And then they despair. They turn to their sleeping men. They say bitterly: *I gave you my dream. What have you done with it? Where did you leave it? At least let me have it back.*'

All this the teacher shouted. I'd never heard anything like it, someone shouting for that long.

'What are you talking about? I haven't understood a word,' I said.

'Women stuck with men who don't understand.'

He stepped forward and I matched him backwards. 'Teacher, you carry a big weight on your shoulders. All the women of the world. Small wonder you're agitated.'

He still moved. I was running out of steps back.

'Let's do this trial,' I said. 'Let's do it now.'

The Accusation

The teacher backed off when I said that. 'You'll get your trial. That's all I wanted. And all the bullshit I had to listen to.' He grabbed a few rocks and placed them in a line between us.

'Let us play out another historical drama, you and I.'

'And that would be? Another battle, another of your obscure incidents, a minor calamity? Am I on the right side this time?'

'As long as you tell the truth, yes you can be.'

'The truth? You mean what happened?'

'Yes.'

'If I can remember it. If it's something I learned.'

'You'll know this one. I guarantee it.'

'So what are we going to act out?'

'A trial.'

'Oh, this is it then? And whose trial?'

'Yours.'

'What for? What's this about?'

'Your guilt.'

He was losing the run of himself, I thought. Cracking. Wonder he'd held out so long. Pressure could get to the best. Bombs, bullets, corpses, burning buildings.

'What guilt?' I said. 'I stole a sweet when I was twelve. I

flung a stone into a crowd of boys at school and ducked when they looked around. I worked hard all my life to get to where I am.'

'The trial is about establishing your guilt in a proper courtroom in front of a judge and jury and a gallery of your peers. The world's cameras.' He smiled and rose a bent finger to his right eye as if holding a camera. 'Flash flash,' he said. 'Smile now. Flash!'

He stood formally as if behind a dais and said, 'All rise for the Honourable.' Then the teacher turned in one complete revolution and said in an elevated, officious tone, 'Will the prosecutor read out the charge?' He turned in another circle and said:

'In the weeks preceding the attack on our town, fearful of an invasion and the destruction of his business, the baker left for the border area and contacted the enemy when the border battle was in progress. After promises of safety, he told them the best way and time to attack the town. They sent him plans to build two ovens in his back garden, one a harmless decoy, the other considerably bigger. Both ovens were built in the second week of November, two weeks before the enemy attacked. He built the first oven on his own. They secretly assisted him in the building of the second oven. Trial witnesses will testify that, on the night of the actual attack two weeks later, plain-clothes strangers visited the baker's house with black plastic bags that required two men to lift.'

'Rubbish.'

'That's why the baker's name was top of the list. That's why they visited him first. The baker was an active collaborator.'

'Rubbish.'

'His shop escaped damage in the fighting.'

'Luck.'

'And we believe we can form a theory, not yet proven, we admit, that will determine the events in the baker's garden on the days in question.'

'I built an oven. Everybody knows I built an oven.'

The Trial Begins

'But Baker, you built another oven, didn't you?'

'That's a question, not a charge,' I said.

'Is that an objection?'

'Are you the teacher or the prosecutor?'

'I am the judge at this moment,' said the teacher.

'Judge, I act in my own defence. I am the baker.'

'Very well,' said the teacher-judge-prosecutor.

'Look, this is unfair. I should be the judge to even things out,' I said.

'Defendant and judge at the same time?' he said.

'Well you are the prosecutor and judge and all the witnesses against me.'

'You can't be defendant and judge at the same time,' he said.

'Why not? A judge is supposed to be neutral. Not supposed to care who wins or loses.'

'Very well, you be the judge.'

'Thank you,' I said. 'And as the judge, I sustain the baker's objection.'

The prosecutor said, 'Let me rephrase, Your Honour. We charge that the baker who stands before us built a second, larger oven in anticipation of or during the recent period of occupation.'

'Your plea?' I asked.

'I don't know really,' I responded as the defendant.

'Use yes or no,' I said.

'I'm sorry, Your Honour,' I said. 'No.'

'Thank you,' I said.

'I call our first witness,' said the teacher.

'Proceed.'

The teacher whispered, 'I have to be all the witnesses. You can't be a witness against yourself.'

That seemed logical. Anyway, I wouldn't want to have to tell what I knew.

'Swear in the Shoemaker,' I said.

The shoemaker was duly sworn in and took his stand at the edge of the hole.

The teacher said, 'You live in the same terraced row as the Baker, is that not correct?'

THE SHOEMAKER: Yes.

'Mr Shoemaker, tell us what you observed during the second week of November.'

THE SHOEMAKER: You mean this year?

'Yes.'

THE SHOEMAKER: I saw unusual activity at the Baker's house.

'And how would you characterize this unusual activity?'

THE SHOEMAKER: Wait, consulting my notes. I made notes, you see.

Nosey bastard, I whispered.

The judge said, 'Did that comment come from inside the courtroom?'

'I heard it too,' I said. 'Disgraceful, Your Honour.'

'Please continue,' I said.

THE SHOEMAKER: I saw a big convoy come to the Baker's house early one morning. A truckload of mortar mix, shovels, and plywood, and two truckloads of mortar and firebricks.

'Who unloaded the materials from said trucks?'

The shoemaker flipped through his pages.

THE SHOEMAKER: Page two.

'What?'

THE SHOEMAKER: Of my notes.

And everyone waited.

THE SHOEMAKER: Men in plain clothes acted like soldiers. Probably soldiers.

'Anything else?' asked the prosecutor.

THE SHOEMAKER: Don't believe so.

'Thank you.'

The judge asked me, 'Cross?'

'No. The notebook wouldn't answer anyway.'

The prosecutor rose again, 'I call the Cleaning Lady.'

She was duly sworn.

THE CLEANING LADY: It was a Friday actually. I was doing a job at this new house, cleaning the windows to earn some extra money even though I should have been out with the rest of the young people drinking and having a good time, well not that they were either but you know what I mean—

'Please get to the point,' the judge said.

THE CLEANING LADY: I saw you, not the judge, the Baker I mean, building a big oven, much bigger than the first one, the small one. This was about five metres long by two-and-a-half wide. Huge hearth. Don't know what you were planning to bake for, a whole battalion, maybe. Saw you from the high windows of the house two doors down from yours. Saw everything. The men helped you. And I can tell you I polished those windows till I near wore them out! Don't go suggesting they weren't clean. I could see you! Yes!

She pointed to me.

'The witness is excused,' the judge said.

'Cross examination!' I urged.

'Go ahead,' I said to myself.

I turned to the cleaning lady.

'Could you tell the court where you were on the evening of Wednesday the second of February at four thirty-five in the afternoon?'

THE CLEANING LADY: Wednesdays I do a half day. I'm sure I was cleaning though, no, that would have been the morning.

'I ask again, what were you doing?'

THE CLEANING LADY: So long ago, I can't really remember.

'You can't remember, is that it?' I said in a crescendo.

THE CLEANING LADY: Yes, and don't shout at me, young man.

'And last week on Wednesday morning at ten forty, what were you thinking?'

THE CLEANING LADY: The usual stuff, I suppose.

'What is the usual stuff? Food? Cards? Vodka?'

THE CLEANING LADY: No, you cheeky man! Just the usual things I think about, same as anyone else.

I try to sound bored: 'What . . . were . . . you . . . thinking?'

THE CLEANING LADY: I don't know.

'So you admit you can't remember what you were doing or thinking on two separate Wednesdays of this year?'

THE CLEANING LADY: That's—

'Thank you,' I said with the 'you' inflected upward as a dismissive send-off, and I turned my back on her. I spoke courteously to the judge:

'No more questions, Your Honour. No evidence of a so-called "second oven".'

The judge said, 'The prosecution's next witness.'

'The blackbird will take the stand, with Your Honour's permission.'

The blackbird took the stand and was duly sworn.

The prosecutor asked, 'What did you see on the day in question?'

THE BLACKBIRD: About two weeks before the battle here, I saw this man out building at night with a string of four blue lights hanging from extension wires. I wondered what he was building. Banging, sawing. Papers with drawings on them. He hasn't any children; I've never seen the neighbours' children in or anywhere near his house, they're scared of him. It was a big project, one he was proud of. Kept talking to the strange men helping him about how he had built a smaller oven in two days, the 'heat-retaining masonry oven'. No wonder he wasn't afraid of getting shot. On the same night the town was attacked, I saw smoke coming out the pipe of the big oven.

'Smoke?'

THE BLACKBIRD: Smoke.

'No more questions.'

'Defendant?' asked the judge.

'No questions for the blackbird apart from the observation that it is a blackbird.'

THE BLACKBIRD: I heard that. I hear things and I see things. When the fighting came to the town, I saw and heard a lot of noise, cannon, firing, half-empty and everyone hiding. I saw where they hid. I see well in winter, bare branches, you see. And I saw men dragging and lifting black plastic bags into the Baker's back garden, yes, yours, in the dead of night.

Next to take the witness box was the cat, who was asked the same questions.

THE CAT: I know what I saw. He built something, that's all I'll say. Threw a stone at me, he did. And my name is Buddy.

At this point the prosecutor had to go to the toilet. When he had finished, he introduced more eyewitness evidence. People I'd never heard of.

'Witnesses have reported a truckload of concrete mix, two truckloads of bricks. Interesting. Comment, defendant?'

'Nothing to add to that lie,' I said. 'Maybe the next one.'

'Baker, your house is terraced, so this was hardly an extension going on. Patio for your plants to thrive in? I don't think so. Smoke. That's what people reported. Smoke above the tree line. Smoke above the trees on the second day after you built the second oven.' He slowed for the last two words.

'Look,' I said. 'Trees surround my back garden. No one can see what I do in my back yard. The smoke was from the only oven I built, a small oven.'

'No, No!' the prosecutor said, and to my surprise the judge made no attempt to act on what was obvious harassment.

The prosecutor said, 'You built another oven, a bigger one, after the first. Didn't you!'

'NO NO NO,' I said in a bored voice, each word a different musical note.

'So everyone in this court is lying?'

'Yes.'

'The Shoemaker is lying?'

'Yes.'

'The Cleaning Lady?'

'Especially the Cleaning Lady.'

'The blackbird?'

'Yes, a wonder he's even taken seriously at all.'

'The cat?'

'The cat too.'

THE CAT: My name is Buddy.

Round two produced deeper questions for the defendant on philosophical grounds.

'The philosophical questioning will begin,' I said (as the judge). 'Well, prosecutor?'

'Your Honour, permission to treat the defendant as a hostile witness?'

'Granted.'

Hostile witness! Had I just done that to myself? Yes, well, got to keep up appearances at least.

'Have you killed people in the last ten days?'

'Not a philosophical question, that one,' I said as the defendant.

'Answer the question!' I said as the judge.

'Killed people? Most certainly not.'

'What is your definition of murder?'

'Killing someone.'

'Are you aware that it evolved from early German usage that meant *killing in secret* as opposed to doing it in the open?'

'No.'

'If you didn't know that, then you made no distinction
between the two.'

'Correct.'

'Can you understand why they made this distinction?'

'No.'

'Then I must ask you, Baker, whether you have murdered anyone in the last two days.'

'No, I have not.'

'Very well. You state that you have not murdered anyone.'

'Yes.'

'In the last two days.'

'Yes.'

He turned.

'And before that?'

'No.'

'Have you facilitated murder?'

'No. I bake every day, and very recently, meaning this
morning, I have been made to dig a hole.'

'Have you assisted the invasion forces?'

'No. I just did what they told me to do.'

'So you assisted them.'

'I had to do what they told me.'

'No, you didn't.'

'I wanted to live. I have a right to live. By doing what
they told me to, I kept myself alive. Self-preservation cannot
be a crime.'

'Only when it leads to others losing their lives, surely.'

'No. Unless you are willing to take that logic the whole
way.'

'I don't understand your response.'

'I'll explain my response. It's been raining all week. The
river rages through the town. A child falls in and is carried

along at speed towards the bridge and the open sea. If you don't jump into the river to rescue the child, are you guilty of assisting in its death?'

'No.'

'But you could have jumped in.'

'Possibly.'

'And you didn't. Because you might drown. Self-preservation.'

'I ask the questions,' said the prosecutor.

'Prosecutor, stick to the philosophical enquiry,' said the judge.

I resented that intrusion just when I was getting the upper hand. These judges! Higher and mightier than the rest of us.

The prosecutor folded his hands behind his back and announced in a dramatic tone, 'Very well, then. Have it your own way. I recall the cat!'

'Oh good Jesus,' said the cat.

I watched the cat take the witness stand. Folded my arms and sighed.

The prosecutor said, 'I apologize for the recall. I must ask you to enlarge on your testimony regarding what you saw in the Baker's back yard on the day or days in question.'

THE CAT: He was building an oven.

'How big was it?'

THE CAT: I didn't have my ruler with me.

'Bigger than a normal oven?'

THE CAT: How big would that be?

'Bigger than a normal oven.'

THE CAT: How big is normal?

'An outdoor oven? Something along those lines.'

THE CAT: How far can a dog run into a wood?

The judge interrupted, 'That's a nonsensical question and completely irrelevant and you don't get to ask questions.'

THE CAT: How long?

'I don't know,' the prosecutor said.

THE CAT: Half way; then she's running out of the wood. And you don't need to measure anything to be right about that. It's just accepted.

'Ah, excellent.'

THE CAT: That's how big the oven was. It was bigger than a normal oven.

'I see.'

THE CAT: And my name is Buddy.

'Thank you, Mr Buddy.'

The prosecutor rubbed his hands across his cheeks as the judge called for a five-minute recess. After the break, the prosecutor asked for permission to include new evidence of a philosophical nature.

After some discussion at the side bar, the judge agreed. Everyone took a seat.

'Baker,' said the prosecutor, 'have you ever heard of a gentleman by the name of JOHN LOCKE?' He shouted the name and a piece of his spit missed my face. Waved sheets of paper around in the air.

THE EVIDENCE ACCORDING TO
JOHN LOCKE

'I object,' I said. 'This evidence presumably already existed and should have been made available under discovery.'

'Overruled,' I said to myself.

'Well?' the prosecutor leered, and he leaned forward so that his breath congealed in my nostrils and made me taste his breakfast.

'Never even heard of him. That good enough for you?'

He said, 'Then you'll never have heard of the blank slate.'

'Nope.'

'*Tabula rasa.*'

I said, 'Haven't heard of that, either.'

'Then I'm sure you won't be able to explain what it means to the good people of this court.'

'Haven't read about it, so how could I?'

The prosecutor turned to the judge with a flourish.

'Your Honour, the People wish to enter the philosophy of John Locke into evidence.'

'Mark it as Prosecution Exhibit 00001-01,' I said dryly.

Someone coughed. I think it was me.

'Was that a comment or a cough?' asked the judge.

Rising, I coughed again, thinking *Who the hell is John Locke?* but saying, 'What are the qualifications of this evidence? Is this an expert piece of evidence?'

'What's that?' they said together.

'Is the evidence a recognized authority?' I scrambled for the right words based on what I'd heard of trials.

'You mean, is John Locke a recognized authority?'

'Yes.'

The prosecutor turned to the judge.

'Your Honour, may I enter into the records a brief history of John Locke in order to establish his credentials for this hearing?'

'You may.'

'John Locke, philosopher, natural scientist, investigator of the human mind. Born 1632 in England, died 1704 in England. Helped lay the philosophical groundwork for the Enlightenment in England and France, influenced the US Constitution. His greatest work is an essay on how humans can understand or know things. During his travels through France from 1675 to 1679 he wrote pieces on botany, medicine, statistics, zoology, instruments, and the weather. He spent the years 1683 to 1689 as an exile in Holland, where he wrote his *Letter concerning Toleration*. In 1685 the English government named him as a wanted traitor—'

'Enough,' I said as the judge. 'Enough qualifications have been presented, I mean.'

The prosecutor said, 'Then may I continue with presenting the evidence?'

'Yes.'

Smiling, the prosecutor said to no one in particular, 'You will notice the sentence that reads thus on the page marked A-1: "Humanity is a blank slate".'

'A black state?' I asked (as the judge).

'A blank slate. Can you hear me, Your Honour?'

'The wind is getting louder, Mr Prosecution.'

'A blank slate, or *tabula rasa*.' Louder now.

'Continue.'

The prosecutor said, 'It is Locke's theory of knowledge and therefore of psychology. How we know things, in layman's terms.'

'Know what?' Judge again.

'When you look out of a window, Your Honour, how do you know that it is a tree you see? How is it that you believe some things are moral and other things immoral?'

'Very well, continue,' I said as the judge.

As the defendant who wanted to appear nonchalant, I could see that the prosecutor enjoyed himself with all this evidence piled up in his folders waiting to explode in my face like an avalanche. Taking his time. Holding a match to the cannon. Smug bastard.

The prosecutor went on, 'Locke was not, however, the originator of this idea. Thousands of years before Locke, Aristotle and indeed the Stoics believed that although the mind was blank at birth, it absorbed information from the five senses and mixed that information with a hibernating intellectual system and made knowledge out of it. Sort of like baking bread, Your Honour.'

I sighed as the defendant. Pincer movement coming. Sometimes you can see it coming and you have to sit and wait for the collision. *Never a break. Never a break.*

The prosecutor went on, 'But for the real meat we must go forward in time to two thousand years later; Locke, in 1690, wrote in his *Essay concerning Human Understanding*, a copy of which I hold in my hand,' and he waved it in the air, 'that at birth the mind is a blank white paper and that all the materials of reason and knowledge come to the mind through observation and reflection. In this he opposed Descartes, who believed that we are born with a mental package, complete with understanding.'

'To hell with Descartes,' I said.

'What do you mean?' I asked as the judge asking myself, the defendant.

'I could never like him, no matter what he wrote. I was born hating Descartes.'

I adjusted my robes, 'The defendant will refrain from being sarcastic.' I turned to the prosecutor.

'Clarify. You use extremely big words.'

'I am pleased, Your Honour. Locke believed that if we know nothing at birth, then all our moral values come from experiences of pain or pleasure. What is good is whatever gives pleasure. The mind calls bad whatever causes pain. Nothing else. No one is born good or bad. No one is born a devil or a dictator.'

'That's interesting,' I said. 'I could agree with that.'

'And furthermore, Locke's ultimate moral conclusion is that, since we are not born good or bad, our moral sense is constructed entirely from our environment. What we see, hear, taste, touch, smell. We are moral creatures of our senses.'

'Yes,' said the judge, 'I understand. Continue.'

'And so, if I may address the court in general, Locke further believed that education was critical as it promoted rational moral values as opposed to irrational values, those based on superstition or religious belief. Schools should not instil faulty thinking in students. Schools should teach them *how*, not *what* to think.'

'Wait a minute,' I said as the defendant, rising.

'I will finish,' said the prosecutor.

The judge nodded, and the prosecutor continued, 'Locke argued for tolerance, since we are what we have experienced.'

'That's enough,' I said. 'I mean, objection! Prosecution is making a speech!'

The judge said, 'You are wandering, counsel. Objection is sustained. Get to the point.'

The prosecutor said, 'Very well, Your Honour.' He took a breath, approached me.

A bit too close.

'Now, defendant, does the evidence I have presented the court about the senses and knowledge suggest to you that Locke believed all of what we know comes from perception?'

'Appears so.'

'Yes or no?'

'Yes.'

'That what we call intuition is really a heap of impressions piled so deep in our minds that we can't access it any more, only feel its murky depths – shapes, words, colours, ideas, fears, impressions, etc.?'

'Yes.'

'Things we call instinct?'

'I don't know if Locke said that or not.'

'So that, therefore, we could not imagine something that is not made up of something we've already seen, heard, tasted, smelt, touched?'

'Maybe.'

'Yes or no?'

'Maybe.'

'Yes or NO!'

'I haven't answered this kind of question before, so I don't know what yes or no would mean as an answer. Locke would support me on that.'

'You must know what murder is if you denied it.'

'Yes.'

'You knew the people who have disappeared?'

'Yes.'

'They were last seen entering your garden.'

'I didn't say that.'

'And smoke rose from the treetops shortly thereafter!'

'I don't know anything about that.'

'And you are a baker and you built an outdoor oven?'

'Yes.'

'With the instructions provided?'

'Yes.'

'So you could have built a replica on a bigger scale?'

'Yes.'

'Did you?'

'No.'

'Enough of these lies! I recall the Shoemaker!'

'Objection!' I shouted.

'Denied!' I shouted.

Everyone scribbled as the shoemaker hobbled to the front of the court.

THE SHOEMAKER: (raised his right hand) I do.

'Please be seated.'

The prosecution said, 'Mr Shoemaker, on the day or days in question, you say you saw mortar, bricks, building materials, trucks and soldiers outside the Baker's house. Correct?'

THE SHOEMAKER: Yes.

'Have you ever seen these items together or separately before?'

THE SHOEMAKER: Yes, many times.

'So that's why you knew what they were?'

THE SHOEMAKER: Yes.

'You did not rely on your memory when you saw them. You recognized them. Is that the word you'd use?'

'Leading question,' I said.

'Sustained,' said the judge.

'Very well. What word would you use?'

THE SHOEMAKER: I recognized the building products and trucks.

'This isn't an interpretation on your part? For instance, maybe they were only similar to those items but were actually daffodils or bicycles.'

THE SHOEMAKER: They were not daffodils and I own a bicycle.

'Were they star constellations?'

THE SHOEMAKER: No.

'Toilet bowls?'

THE SHOEMAKER: No, not those.

'And finally, and thank you for your patience, were they like chewing gum?'

THE SHOEMAKER: No.

'And is it true that from an early age you have been taught that certain words correspond to particular objects?'

THE SHOEMAKER: Yes.

'And the teaching books matched the pictures and words correctly.'

THE SHOEMAKER: I think so . . .

'Back to the garden. Did you see the Baker on the night in question?'

THE SHOEMAKER: Yes, he was scurrying around—

'Objec—'

'Sustained! The witness will rephrase, please.'

THE SHOEMAKER: He carried some of the lighter tools into the garden from the trucks. The men carried the heavier things, like bricks and mortar mix.

'Did you recognize the garden as being, in fact, a garden?'

THE SHOEMAKER: I have a garden and all the elements of a garden were there. It was behind the house and it had grass and a path to a shed at the back wall.

'Thank you. No more questions for this witness.'

'Cross-examination?' asked the judge.

'A few questions,' I said.

'Proceed.'

'Thank you,' I said to myself. 'Mr Shoemaker, how would you describe your relationship with your wife?'

The prosecutor jumped to his feet with his finger stuck to the ceiling and his mouth open. He must have seen where I was going but I had the judge on my side with this one.

'Sit down,' said the judge, looked at his watch and turned to the shoemaker. 'Answer the question, please. Briefly. I'm hungry.'

THE SHOEMAKER: We've been married twenty-three years. It's a happy marriage.

'Interesting,' I said. 'You just used one word to describe a twenty-three-year phenomenon, namely your marriage, but you went into significant detail when describing what you thought was a short unloading of materials from a couple of trucks at one thirty in the morning outside my house.'

THE SHOEMAKER: Was it one thirty?

'Did I say that? I don't know,' I said. 'How many times have you been married to your wife for twenty-three years?'

THE SHOEMAKER: Once, I think.

'Once. How interesting. Then how do you know it's a happy marriage, as opposed to any other type? You have nothing to compare it with in your experiences. You've only been married to her once, by your own admission.'

THE SHOEMAKER: I suppose so.

'And if your opinion is faulty on such an intimate subject as your marriage, how can we be sure of your accuracy based on a fleeting glimpse of me in the early hours?'

THE SHOEMAKER: I don't know . . . married once only.

I smiled as the prosecutor fumed. Hung him on his own petard. The John Locke reverse stranglehold.

'I have no more questions.'

The judge dismissed the shoemaker, who rose with a foolish look on his face.

'So therefore,' I said to no one in particular (borrowing the prosecutor's ploy), 'we have a man, who can't make out what's in front of him and who can't properly evaluate his own marriage, claiming to have seen various particulars, bricks, mortar, trucks, in a dark place situated thirty odd metres from his window at night, when he was probably exhausted anyway. Come to your own conclusions.'

The prosecutor said, 'My last witness is the defendant.'

'Very well. Will the defendant take the witness stand? Prosecutor, conclude the philosophical examination, please. It's getting close to lunchtime.'

'Permission to include a moral component in the questioning,' asked the prosecutor.

'Granted. But be careful, counsel. I'll be watching. Don't stray.'

The prosecutor smiled at me, his head cocked as if listening to something only he could hear. Knifefuls of sarcasm.

'You know, I have to ask this,' he said. 'Who got to you? Who did something that made you this way? A father? An uncle? A friend at school? A stranger in a bus shelter showed you some pictures? Or is the unthinkable a possibility?'

'I don't have to answer any of that. I don't think—'

The prosecutor said, 'Answer the question!'

'—so.'

'Answer the question, prisoner in the dock! Prisoner with the guilty frown!'

'What fucking question!'

'The possibility that you were born evil. Did the darkness itself reach out and touch you with its icy fingers before you even left the womb? What should we do with you?'

'I'm not an expert on the unborn and I don't know what you mean when you say Evil and I'm not a judge. You confuse me.'

The prosecutor continued, 'Should we detect people such as you at birth and terminate you? Why wait for you to do your work?'

From the spectator seats, a shrill voice:

THE CLEANING LADY: I didn't come here to listen to that kind of talk. I think abortion is terrible, murder, killing a little child like that.

'Shut up,' said the judge.

THE CLEANING LADY: You think I'm not as educated as you, is that it? Does that give you the right—

'Shut up and sit down,' said the judge.

THE CLEANING LADY: —to decide that what I say is less valuable than what you say?

'I said Shut up and now I'm saying Shut up.'

Silence as the cleaning lady decided not to say anything. I played with an imaginary pencil until the judge cleared his throat.

'Go on, please. Defendant, you were giving evidence, I believe.'

I said, 'I haven't done anything except what I was made do at gunpoint. If that's my crime then you must accuse others from this town along with me. The Shoemaker will measure the soldiers' feet and make boots for them. People in this town brewed the coffee the soldiers drink in the restaurant. If I didn't bake my bread in the morning, as I had to do this very morning, the soldiers would have beaten me, or worse. Should a town rise in revolt against its occupiers and be judged guilty if it doesn't? Prove that and I'll be impressed. Don't single me out, that's all I'll say. Don't look for a scapegoat.'

The prosecutor said, 'Or perhaps evil is handed down like children's clothes in a poor family. The sins of the father in the genes of the son.'

I said, 'But how could that happen?'

'It's called crossing time and space.'

I said, 'No crossing time and space with anything we don't bring with us.'

The prosecutor said nothing for what lasted a long time then but now seems like a second.

After that silence, the teacher moved forward, said, 'The Trial is over.'

'So I can be myself again.'

'Baker, I suffer from sleep paralysis,' he said.

Ah, indeed, the teacher again. Weak, pathetic, used up.

'The prosecutor has gone home now,' he said, 'You won't hear from him again.'

'That's a relief,' I said. 'I think the judge wanted out as well. Hungry. And what's that thing, sleep paralysis?'

'Strange, frightening. My body freezes. I am awake but can't move. Happens sometimes when I'm about to fall asleep or wake up, sometimes even in my sleep. I dream that I am near waking. The air in the room changes, a presence moves across the dark, a terrible sound in my ear like people talking in a small radio behind the pillow, every time, my God, every single time, this horrible thing happens I try to get up or move a finger or scream, but I can't. I just lie there praying the sheet won't fall across my face and smother me. I am awake, Baker, fully awake and without movement. A weight on my chest, something pressing hard, incredibly evil, a sense, a bad presence in the room, and I can't move. My wife knows nothing of this.'

I asked, 'How long does it last?'

'Sometimes ten, fifteen minutes. I want to scream. Ragged, raw feeling like my consciousness being shaved slice by slice. My body is asleep and I breathe slowly, evenly in spite of my inner turmoil. The badness sits on my chest and moves about the room, at leisure. Sometimes right to left, rarely left to right. I've tried to call out: useless. I lie in terror of suffocating. I focus on my right index finger and try to move it, try to twitch the middle joint so that my nerves will spark or a neuron fire or the match that is energy strike and flame me back into the fire of the living. And for such a long time, Baker, nothing jumps across the divide between my brain and my body. And then, from deep within, a vestige of a signal to my nerves, a message, no, a signal desperately galloping through the fog to the light at the end of the road. And when my movement is restored I rise angrily, recovering from my fear and ask,

Who are you? What do you want? The same questions, over and over.'

'Basic questions,' I said.

'Police have found uninjured people dead with looks of terror on their faces. Across countries and generations, that presence has been called the Old Hag or witch. A medieval woodcut shows a witch sitting on the chest of an armoured knight who lies immobilized on the floor. I can tell you without hesitation that he, the knight, so many hundred years ago, felt the same as I, that I have known his exact terror, across all the time between us, across all of your inventions, Baker, and all of your precious wars.'

'So—' I asked, but he ignored me.

'And though I accept the reality of human contact across time, whether in poetry or direct experience, this paralysis must have some scientific cause.'

'Yes, of course!' I shouted, relieved.

'Some say it's the genes in the body reacting near the boundaries of sleep to early humans' memory of intruders in the black, musty cave. Can you see it? Terror, imminent death, reaching us across a space of hundreds of thousands of years. Perhaps evil is the same. It touches some as an instinct and can't be resisted.'

'Now wait—'

'It visits you all from out of your relatives' deeds, long before you were born; it knocks on the door of your soul and says, *Here I am, and this is what you need to know.* What would we—'

'Yes?' I asked.

'What could we call such an awareness?'

'Mortal terror,' I said. 'I don't know what you're talking about.'

'Baker, evil is what you've done, isn't it?'

'I don't know what you're talking about.'

'Evil evil evil evil.'

'I don't know what you're talking about.'

He fixed me with a hammer-nail of a stare and said, 'I think you do.'

Four Twenty in
the Afternoon

The teacher climbed out of the hole, straightened his clothes, and brushed the snow off his coat. I made a fuss out of cleaning the blade of the shovel but at this time of the day, in this light, not a soul would care if I left my working tool dirty. It was a good Markham shovel, made to last, a few dings along the handle, light, durable. A solid companion for the day's work. They gave it to me, probably took it from a labourer, a bricklayer's server. Better than a simple farmyard shovel, this one.

'It's four twenty,' he said. Made a big show with the watch. 'We're near the end of this business, so we may as well put the icing on the cake. Put it all together for posterity. Final draft.'

I put the shovel down, took the pickaxe, and swung.

'I'm not sure I get your drift.'

'Baker, prepare to hear the judgement of history.'

I leaned on the pickaxe and asked him, 'What will some-one like me be reading about these past few days in fifty years' time?'

His finger pointed up and he strode purposefully for the first time all afternoon.

'We can use Schopenhauer's telescope.'

SCHOPENHAUER'S TELESCOPE

'Schopenhauer's telescope?' I said. 'It's daytime, clouded over. Can't see much now. Where does he live?'

'The great philosopher of the nineteenth century said that to gain perspective on any problem, we should travel fifty odd years into the future and invert a telescope, look through the wrong end, from that time in the future, at ourselves as we are, and make decisions with the benefit of hindsight.'

I said, 'You mean look back at yourself from a time in the future and do whatever the fifty years has taught you about yourself?'

'Right. Now let's use the telescope. Here it is.'

He picked up a frozen stick and held it to his eye.

'Baker,' he said, 'what do we see?'

I pretended to look through a lens.

'Nothing.'

He said, 'I see two men standing by a hole at winter's onset. Serious crimes have been committed. A typed report, the final rendering of judgement on what you did and what I did, this report lies on a shelf, covered in time by reports of other atrocious behaviour.'

'Watch your language.'

'Of other more terrible events.'

'That's better.'

'And now let us open the document.' He mimed tearing an envelope or opening a strap. 'Prepare to hear your fate, Baker.'

I stood sort of to attention and felt foolish. Snow was an inch on my shoulders because I hadn't shovelled for a while. Dangerous not to keep moving in these conditions. Frostbite. Lose your damn fingers and much more.

He read in a voice much too loud, 'Here is the report.'

I said, 'I'm cold.'

'Then I'll skip the introduction.' He cleared his throat, 'Meanwhile, the two countries could not resolve mineral rights at their respective northern borders. Localized fire-fights intensified without governmental restraint or diplomatic contact. Finally, the border conflict spread south. All towns within a radius of fifteen kilometres came under fire from the invading troops, who after two days of vicious fighting, took control of the entire peninsula. A stalemate ensued with minor advances and retreats. Though neither army was particularly well equipped, heavy civilian casualties made this dispute remarkable. The number of civilian dead far exceeded what would be expected in an open-country battleground and in a rural hinterland of relatively isolated towns. Satellite images of gravesites indicated systematic killings of the citizenry by the invading troops. A post-conflict war crimes tribunal failed to identify enough witnesses to piece together a cohesive case, though some isolated south-ern kangaroo courts prosecuted and executed suspected collaborators.'

'Executed?'

'The case of the baker. Case number 00001.'

'What, I'm number one?'

'Isn't it nice to be at the top of the list? Instant fame. Think of it! Hitler, Stalin, Leopold, Khan, The Baker. Oh, children will quake at the knees under the blankets when Daddy says: "Go to sleep or the baker will come and get you; now, child, you don't want that, do you?"'

'They wouldn't talk about me like that! No! I don't believe it for a second.'

'Of course they will. You'll be famous!'

I laughed, kicked at the snow, 'No, that couldn't be. I'm not really that important, am I? Am I?'

'You're terribly important, Baker. May I continue? Thank you. The baker is recorded as having assisted the invading troops in helping them flush out those in hiding, including the policeman and his wife. He claimed that he had acted under duress; yet it was established that the baker approached the occupying forces, without having been threatened even once, and offered them his services. He freely admitted this. Yes, he showed them where the policeman's wife was hiding and watched as they played with her and then shot her. Certain important people, it was explained to him, would have to disappear. The mayor did not turn up for work and was never seen again. The mayor's wife must have gone with him. The doctor was seen being brought away on a truck towards the front. The customary smell of a Havana cigar failed to populate the street outside the retired colonel's bungalow. The retired colonel's housemaid's sister's niece, who had often been seen in the company of the colonel, who liked to tell the young lady stories of an earlier war with the same enemy, appeared to have left with the colonel and the mayor, the mayor's wife, the policeman, and the policeman's wife. The patio of the retired colonel's bungalow could be seen from the window of the baker's house, and it is assumed that the baker gave specific information about comings and goings to enemy intelligence.'

'Wait, this doesn't sound like an official report.'

'In fifty years that is the way they'll write them.'

'Oh,' I said.

'But there is a piece missing from this report.'

I shook my head, 'Yes? I thought you said it was written in hindsight.'

'And so it is. The last piece of information I need from you now. Come on, you've got nothing to lose by telling the truth, have you? I mean, look at the situation.'

He placed the telescope across his shoulder and said, 'What did you do with them?'

How did he know all this? Did the telescope really work? Why hadn't I heard of it? I realized how weak and vulnerable I was in this place, but the telescope was a weapon so terrible that nothing could be invisible.

I gave up inside.

'Teacher, my involvement was small, not much, I mean—'

The teacher said, 'Baker, are you a murderer? Are you like the *traytrous Sonnes, that dy'd by law for the murder of our Brother?*'

He should have let me speak. I said then, 'I don't speak Latin.'

'What have you done to them? About the second oven? Come on!' He screamed and I shook with the ferocity of it.

Evidently the prosecutor was back. I called for the judge.

'I can't help you,' he said.

I walked as far away from the teacher as I could, and still he watched me from the edge.

'You have to believe this,' I said. 'They made me. They said there were people who had to disappear for a while. No evidence. They threatened my life.'

'You had no choice, correct?'

'No choice. They wanted more and more from me. They brought the bodies at night. I lit the ovens and made those people disappear.'

The teacher rubbed his forehead, 'What became of them? Come on, man, get it off your chest. You don't have all that much time to do it.'

I shouted, 'You want to know? What would a professional baker do? I pulverized them into a paste, the bits of them that weren't burned. Spread them around the garden.'

Hush in the gallery.

Although the teacher was clearly at a loss for words, that didn't deter the prosecutor from jumping to his feet.

'My God, that's a war crime!'

'Objection, defence counsel speaking,' I said. 'Citizens can't commit war crimes.'

'Oh yes, they can.'

'Oh no, they can't.'

The judge argued that we leave that point for another hearing. What was important now was that the defence witness, the defendant, had confessed to committing certain practices while under the orders of the occupying force.

The prosecutor shook his head and paced the hole. I strained my neck to keep up with his to and fro until he turned.

'You made dust of them, parts of them,' he said. 'Logical,

I suppose. And what did you do with what you couldn't smash?'

'I hid those parts.'

'Where?'

'They are hidden.'

He roared, 'Where are they, you devil?'

'I don't know and I don't care!'

The teacher butted in without as much as a by-your-leave to the prosecutor, 'I shudder at the horrors that must lie in that shed of yours.'

I said, 'Nothing is in the shed.'

'I'm sure of it. You hardly put them in the house. You wouldn't have done that.'

'All done under orders, but yes, I wanted to understand them. Have them inside me, gain their knowledge. Like people do with Jesus. That's where I got the idea. Knew there had to be something in that stuff, drink his body, blood, that idea. I wanted to learn what I could from the dead. Not sure if Jesus is coming back though. The first fifty years, one hundred, I'd have been looking out the window at night and up the next morning but now, it's been too long. Must like where he is, why would he come back? I say take the best from everyone and expect no return, except what you take.'

'Baker, I have just seen the face of evil. It is like a little boy, harmless in a way that might keep you off guard, who knows everything and understands nothing. And he damages like an insect, invisible, one insect kills a field by eating without stop because the field is passive, there to be eaten. Because the insect is possessed with one purpose. The question is no longer—'

'No longer what?'

'Who is evil or who has this insatiable hunger. The question must be, from where does evil come?'

'Would you want to know?' I asked.

'Why not?'

'Well, what would you do? Say, *Hello, Evil. How's it going? What's new? You're looking awful today?*'

MASKS

I asked myself what I knew about the face of evil. The response I gave myself back mentioned masks.

This is what I know about masks.

I learned about personality from the fashion world on television. I watched those women float down the catwalks and realized something very, very important. That clothes were a mask. And I thought that the best way to live among people when you are not one of them is to wear a perfect mask, so real that it is indistinguishable from your skin. You have to pick carefully, try each one on and walk around in it for at least a day.

See how people react.

Over the months, while deciding on a personality, I tried on various roles and the mask to go with each one. At different times I tested appearances and postures for my customers; I tested haughty, pleasant, impatient, cross, ingratiating, deferential; I tried wringing my hands and smiling at the bakery store customers' infernal pretence at choosing when they were in fact going to buy the same items as they always did! I wanted to flog them with their receipt and ask them if it did or did not list the same item as all the other receipts from my store that they had brought home in the past.

That last bit, my impatience, convinced me that I must cure it with nature.

In the end I chose indifference because I didn't have to act. That's the way I felt, and it was a relief when I could breathe easy and just be myself. Still, I wore the mask all day anyway since the people I had to deal with were insufferable. And occasionally at home, when I drank too much, I went to the bathroom and studied the mask in the mirror, the one I couldn't pull off now, so hard was it stuck, and I tweaked my features, re-assembling an expectant eyebrow, smoothing a wrinkle of impatience on my brow.

At those times I thought that my mask was grafted to my face with the grip of a man hanging off a cliff edge and I'd never get it off. I even tried peeling it and watched the razor carefully as I drew it across my jaw in case it lifted a flap of skin and the real me behind the real me would stare back at the real me in the mirror. Just as well the mask was me. Imagine being one thing and looking like another. I think they call that a split person, that's what I've read, but not memorized, so I can't be sure.

I've been cut enough but I've never split.

I placed objects in the fire for all my adult employment and waited till a crisp tasty loaf filled the air with mouth-watering freshness. All the moments of my undistinguished life led me to this meeting with the teacher. And if I were now the one consumed, I would accept my fate. It was as unavoidable as fire in a dry forest.

That is philosophy for me. What happens, not why.

Less torture that way. No swearing at the crucifix or the oracle, asking why me? As if you were special or deserving of a special mention when billions are thinking the same thing.

Billion people at any one time, say one out of five, asking, 'Why me? or, Why does this always happen to me?' And the oracle says, 'Because it always happens to you, get it? There isn't another way. Who told you there was? Who do you think you are, exactly?'

THE FOURTH TRUCK

The sound of another truck, the smoke from the exhaust, the squeal of brakes, the slide of the huge wheels, a door slams. The truck faced the field, its lights shone like the moon across the snow.

This time the brackets at the rear of the truck squeaked and the tailgate fell.

But no citizens emerged.

Uniformed men jumped out, suspicious, holding their coats closed. Even in this light I could see their grim, clenched jaws when they turned to one another. Oversized eyes.

I felt the fear swim in my stomach.

They moved forward, unsure of footing, rifles held loosely at hip-level, one palm down over the barrel. They looked professional enough to be relaxed under pressure, approached the wall to our field, leaped softly and landed with flat feet, perfectly balanced, heads up and ready. They had seen action. You know the type once you've seen action yourself instead of just reading about it.

Two of them carried a heavy machine gun to the gun emplacement where the two soldiers had waited all afternoon, lifted the plastic cover, and placed it on a tripod. The assistant gunner took off his gloves and fed in an ammunition belt from a green metal case. He had a bandage around his hand with a stain on it like a ring. Then they put the cover back on, smoked, clapped their hands together. The kettle rattled, back on the fire.

The teacher glanced behind him and then faced me.

'Are you ready?' he asked.

'As ready as you are.'

'This evening I might be with my wife, or I may not find her at all,' he said.

'Your wife? What about her? Has anything happened to her?'

'You can't undo what you've done. Not here.'

And then he did something that took me by surprise.

He laughed.

'It doesn't matter,' he said.

I believe there was a reason why, at that moment, the wind died down. The snow still fell, but straight out of the night now. And it took its time now.

A Dialogue About Betrayal

'It doesn't matter,' he said, 'because you'd never learn, even if you lived a thousand years in front of the same page of the same book, your eyes fixed to the same word, and all the world frozen around you, not a sound, not a taste, not a smell.'

I said, 'I know a lot,' and smiled back at him. 'Maybe you fear how much I know.'

Time to be brazen. I took the shovel and held it high in the air.

I said, 'You're avoiding this topic, aren't you?'

He lit another cigarette, probably the fifteenth of the afternoon. I had lost count, to be honest, which troubled me. These things mattered.

He said, 'Not at all,' and threw away the match. 'I have learned about atrocities from you today. In fact, let us compare atrocities, you and I.'

'Another game, even now?'

'No game.'

'What, then?'

'Discuss our differences.'

'Too late, haven't you noticed?'

He ignored me, looked at the cigarette, blew smoke, then spoke.

'You researched the old reliables, Genghis Khan, the rest of them, but I've always thought of the local atrocity. The girl who disappears after being last seen playing in the meadow, the careful man who throws a bag of puppies over the frozen bridge and goes back to slip into a warm bed beside his wife, tells his child the next morning that Santa took them to the North Pole and promised to care for them. The cleric who counts the collection plate full of widows' coins and puts every fourth one in his pocket for cigarettes.' He tapped his pocket then. 'The promise that you will see your dead parents again. The promise that your suffering is noticed and that the abusers will pay by an unseen hand that will somehow make everything right. That I last saw my wife two evenings ago at five minutes past six. We live within sight of this place. I proposed to her under that tree, you know.' He pointed. I did not follow.

'I don't understand,' I said.

The teacher bowed his head.

'You see, even as a student of history, the scale of these other monstrosities you and I have discussed is too large for me to comprehend. A person's mind, I think, was never meant to feel such emotions. At least mine wasn't. Somehow everyone has disappeared. I need a face to see, one I recognize. I can't feel anything otherwise. If history does possess a face, it is worn by the people we love now, their face.'

I waited for him to say, *My Wife*, in vain.

I said, 'That might well be, whatever you are saying now, but I wanted to learn about the big massacres. I've read about them and that's what I think about.'

'Don't get me wrong, Baker. I admire your certainty. I might even envy it.'

'I know you envy my knowledge.'

'Baker, think of the Germans. Flip a coin, and with the Germans it lands on Hitler or Beethoven. The worst and the best, that's the Germans for you. That's probably what the Celts were like too.'

Yes. At last he was talking about something real.

'Imagine a sunset before a battle. The Celts watch the Romans spread in valleys below them in their metallic legions, ten thousand fires that hoist the ancient night to a body-length above ground, and they dream of their children and wives as few can dream in normal life. The mind of the soldier, Baker; just think of it if you can. I don't believe I could live it. Maybe some emotions weren't meant to be experienced at full throttle.'

'What?' I said.

'We can't recover that fierce loneliness. Of living the solitary life. We've grown fat around our habits, our intellectual life is full of information. We're a slow people now. We know a lot.'

He continued, 'People everywhere. In front, behind, above us in planes, under us in tunnels, to all six sides and behind every crack in the horizon, every drawing of the curtains at sunrise. People live in the places you've never even thought of, my friend, the places you'll never visit. In your ear from morning till night, radios, televisions, phones, conversations on the street, how much is this, singing, the bad news, the good news, the money lost, they are in your eye from the second you are born, on your skin, a shoulder against your back in a line at the post office. A car rounding the bend after you. That certain look in the crowd: people like you, Baker, who know a lot. Who want to tell you what they think. You know a lot, don't you?'

I answered in kind, without missing a beat:

'I know a lot more than you.'

He smiled. 'That's all?'

'That's enough.'

'And what,' he said, 'is your verdict on the soldiers who carried out those orders to massacre? What is your verdict on Mr Fievez? Come, Baker, let us resolve this small matter now, hmm?'

The teacher looked behind him, probably at the crowd in their six lines. He watched them closely, as if looking for someone or something he had sought all his life and never really found.

From down in the hole, I could hear them talking, coughing.

'Want another cigarette?' he asked me.

'All soldiers have their orders,' I said. 'Fievez too.'

'And if they didn't carry out those orders, they would be next,' he said.

'They had their families to think of.'

He said, 'I agree. You have to look at the situation on the ground, as it was then.'

'War gets out of hand,' I said, 'even if it hasn't actually become a war yet, one that will be a war later, you know?'

'Of course.'

'People do things because they have to survive somehow, and that's more important than friendship.'

'I'm glad you have explained that to me,' he said.

I don't know why I said this, but the tone in his voice seemed to accept me.

'So you understand why I acted?' I said.

'I understand your point of view. I mean, that's very

academic, what I said just now, so I'll try to just say it the way it is: I think friendship is more important than survival.'

'How could that be?' I asked.

'I couldn't survive without my friends, my loved ones. I wouldn't know how.'

'You'd learn.'

'I wouldn't want to live without them, Baker.'

'You'd learn, believe me. I know.'

'So how did you make contact with the invading forces?' he asked. 'When was Day One?'

'I lay awake at night, as often happens. I don't sleep well. I was reading the newspapers. The trouble at the border, the build-up. Our side's weakness. I got worried about the shop, there in my bed. All my work could be in vain.'

'Were you always alone at night?'

'Yes, lonely nights, cold wet evenings with nothing to do but read. But I did read. And what was useful to me, what saved my life. So I called and made contact that way. I offered my services.'

'You offered?'

'I let it be known that I could be of service.'

'So you confess, Baker, even at this late hour.'

'Very well then, I confess. Now do you feel any better? But you'll get no apologies from me.'

No Time for Hope Now

The falling snow seemed harmless without the wind. Dainty fat flakes lived a short life before they disappeared into all the others that had fallen before them. We hadn't got used to not having to shout any more, so when the teacher spoke, his voice reverberated in the hole and made me cringe:

'I may have a wife somewhere in those lines, but I can't see her, or any woman.' Then he looked at me, 'Have you ever been married?'

'I never married. I saw no reason to get married,' I said.

He said more, then, as if making up for all of the silence in his life. He said something about hope, but I said there was no time for hope now.

'None?' he asked.

'Very little,' I said.

He lit another cigarette with difficulty. That wind still managed a few gusts, I can't tell you how it must have stabbed him, standing there exposed with nothing between him and it but a coat and a shirt. The matches kept going out on him.

When he finally managed to light the cigarette he took a long drag. 'You've done well out of the occupation,' he straightened his tie, 'until now, that is.'

'Save your judgement. We've got enough in this field already as it is, thank you.'

'Judgement? No judgements here,' he said. 'This is all about the business of nation building. Can't get in the way of that, can we?'

'I wouldn't know anything about nation building. I am a baker by trade.'

'I wanted to be first here,' he said. 'I wanted to talk to you first, maybe understand what lies in that mind.'

'And what have you learned?' I asked, pleased at giving him back his own words like that.

'You are like your brother, you know,' he said.

'I am not. I am not!' I shouted.

'He hadn't an ounce of compassion in his body from the day he was born. Someone forgot to add it to the mix.'

'My brother is a respected—'

I said a lot in a short few seconds.

He didn't listen to a word of it. His eyes back on the crowd, searching. 'She might be in that line.'

'Look carefully. Do you see any women in those lines?' I said.

'Maybe,' he said. 'I haven't seen her for two days. But someone told me yesterday that he had seen her.'

'Good,' I said.

And he snapped. 'Say *Good* again and you'll die saying it.'

Safe in the Hole

The teacher sat on his rock and draped his coat over his head. From their position the soldiers would not make him out. He motioned me over to him with his index finger, and I moved as if on a string attached to it. I stood under his feet, my neck arched to the dark features inside the coat that flapped every now and then.

'After all your study, tell me this, Baker.'

'Tell you what?'

'Tell me what have you learned about love,' he said.

I folded my arms and glanced around the hole until I felt comfortable enough to answer, 'Nothing that I can use.'

'Nothing that you can use, how interesting.' The coat moved. The snow fell. That's all that was happening in the world at that moment, that's how still everything seemed after the storm. Even the teacher and I were like statues in an empty weekend house in the country or out in a big garden by a cold lake.

'You have been very generous with your time today,' he said. 'And now I have a favour to ask of you.'

'I suppose. What is it?'

'Baker, can I tell you a story about love?'

'What can love do in a place like this?' I said. 'What's the point?' I turned my head. 'Look over your shoulder. They're not here to pick flowers. That crowd is not here for a cocktail party. We are way over time, teacher.'

'We have some time, not much, it's half past four.'

'That's late, very late,' I said.

'You are still in the hole, aren't you?'

'Yes, you know I am.'

'Well, nothing will happen until you get out of that hole. Nothing.'

He was right. Climbing out would officially mean the hole was dug. Nothing to lose. I sat against the side of the hole and hunched up.

'Okay,' I said, 'tell me your story about love, but make sure it actually happened, please.'

'It is all fact, and I believe that Genghis Khan himself would pause and wonder at the power of it.'

'Don't put yourself under that kind of pressure,' I said. 'That's big competition for such a little thing that never got anyone anywhere, at least not some people.'

'It's a love story about my wife.' The coat was perfectly still. The teacher held his head straight. I kept still too so I wouldn't betray any hint of interest in his love story.

THAT'S THE WORLD-SHATTERING EVENT THAT TAUGHT YOU ABOUT LOVE?

'What I am about to tell you happened a long time ago, we were married less than a year,' he said. 'We arranged to meet after I had read my students' essays, and we ran on the track, on a sunny morning when the warm air blew on our faces and children played in the park. I dressed in my running clothes and went to the track and saw the bag of fruits and vegetables she had brought from the market on the seats. In the field surrounded by the track, sprinklers arched spurts of water like silver bows bent down to the grass, and I searched until I saw her, rounding the corner in her training pants with small, perfect steps, her belly bare and her blonde hair a fire behind her in the breeze. Her smile answered my wave. I joined her in step and our arms touched and the contact burned into desire between my legs.

'I don't know how the feeling I had next came. To me she was fragrance without a body, movement without muscle, a soul without strings, and I wanted to cry for love and not know why. She made me a child again, you see. This was her gift. But nothing could have prepared me for what happened then, on that ordinary morning in a small town, when I joined my wife on the running track.'

I imagined the teacher's face a blank slate in the early evening. But I was not looking at him any more. His voice – tired, I thought – drifted into the hole.

He said, 'I had loved her for such a long time. I'd never understood what love was, but I felt it. All history taught me was facts and dates, but nothing about what men and women call love. Do you know what I mean?'

I shrugged, lifted my eyebrows.

He said, 'I doubt that you do, but I am trained to hope that you will.'

'Don't hope too much, Teacher.'

'I was twenty-one and a virgin,' he said. 'My parents protected me from the world I had studied so diligently in university. The world to me was something I knew very well and not at all. I knew what love was supposed to be. I could list its symptoms. Lack of sleep, a feeling called desire that ran through the body and into the night and into the hours of each day, tears, unbearable absence, shaking of the body in joy and anticipation. And I knew from the history of conflict that when nothing came of the chase, spurned men pushed large ships into the water and went to war.'

'And history is so much about war,' I said.

'Yes, Baker, I was an expert in the theory of love, but I did not know what it would be like when love came to me, or if it ever would come. I needed more, like the innocent country girl who is promised a beautiful boy to wed but has never seen a picture of the boy. So I did what I was trained to do: I researched. I consulted the great poets, Donne, Catullus, Sappho, read their verse into my blood to give me confidence and a kind of free experience. I will never forget the moment I found John

Donne's poem *The Good Morrow*, where he wakes with his lover and realizes that a whole world has opened up to him:

> *'For love, all love of other sights controls*
> *And makes one little room an everywhere.*

'Or the verse from his "Nocturnal on St Lucy's Day", the shortest day, when his love and he made up the entire universe:

> *'Oft a flood have we two wept, and so*
> *Drown'd the whole world, us two.*

'I consulted *The Book of Good Love* by Juan Ruiz, a thirteenth-century Spanish poet and musician who spent thirteen years in prison, where he revised his masterpiece while remembering his past loves. What experience the good man gave me! And all at no expense other than my time, and that well spent, for I leaped forward, it seemed to me, a year for every minute I read from all these great poems on love.

'Before I even had a girlfriend, I had learned the beginnings and the end of love from Catullus, the greatest lyric poet in Latin literature, who rebuked himself for falling in love:

> *'Open your eyes, you idiot, innocent boy, look what*
> *has happened:*
> *Now she's no longer yielding: you must be, poor idiot,*
> *more like a man! Not running after her,*
> *your mind all tears.*

'But I had no time for losing love, so pure its first effects on me through all the disillusionment and cynicism. I read the rhymes of Francis Petrarch, finding the verses that matched my own feeling:

> 'The eyes I spoke of once in words that burn,
> the arms and hands and feet and lovely face
> that took me from myself for such a space
> of time, and marked me out from other men.

'I bought flowers and filled my bedroom with them so that both the morning and night windows were touched with colour and scent. I bought plants, dark green and full of earth, faced my bed east and then north so that I might sleep better. But still she came in my dreams and took even my rest away. Her face took my breath, her thighs my sight, her feet my fingers, until I lay a sick man, sick with desire and feeling and nothing else, because I was transformed into desire and lost my body. I wanted to lie on her, naked, and kiss her soft lips and speak to her clear blue eyes.

'But I could not move, because my body in my dream was gone.

'I wanted to live with her in a country house bordered with fields of golden corn and wildflower meadows, and walk our daughter and help her fill the world with her imagination.

'But I could not live that, because in the dream my future had vanished.

'There was only the absence of this girl; yet even her presence, when we met, burned me too. I could not be satisfied when she was with me and when she was gone. It was the hell of constant want and with no water to quench it.

'And I realized that love had made me run to my books, knowing all the time that I would not find it there. It was behind me, pushing me with its promise, filling me with its thoughts, deafening me with its laughter and tears.

'I knew then that love maddens men and women because it will not stand before them and say, *Here I am. Know me.* It is a shadow, something that changes the leaves on the trees, the sky's blue, the habitual journey. Love walked behind me like a starved dog in an alley, but I lived better in the world because of love.

'My step fell lighter. My heart lightened and I was happier. My friends drew nearer to me, marvelling at my natural joy and new simplicity.

'I went to study again, but this time I knew better than to chase the science of love or find its formula just so that I could retreat again to my intellect and be at peace.'

He paused, and I shook my head, 'You have spoken now for a few minutes, without interruption.'

'I have.'

'But you forgot something,' I said.

'What?'

I sighed, put my head in my hands, and spoke as loudly as I dared.

'What happened the morning you met your wife on the running track? What happened that could have been more important than all the philosophy in the world, all the facts that man has accumulated? What happened?' I placed a hand under my chin. 'Are you withholding the last, most important part of your lesson because I sit helpless down here and you tower eloquently up there? Is that to be my torture?'

I spoke this way because I had read the great orators. I knew how to tilt a sentence upward at the end and gesticulate with the arm.

The teacher said, 'I will not leave you without the answer to your question,' and he continued as if to unburden himself was the only desire he could feel any more.

'The morning my wife and I ran together turned out to be the hottest day of the summer. We ran slowly, speaking little. After two or three miles, the humidity had drenched us. She called out that she was running under the sprinklers and asked me to come with her, to run with her through the water. She laughed and reached and took my arm and pulled me with her. I let her run ahead and watched her bounce through the stream of water. She danced, bent her body at the hip this way and that, a flower in a breeze. She called to me again because I was shy then; and I ran through the water's cold blunt blade across my back and after her through another sprinkler. And then this wonderful moment poured into my life like a perfumed tea on a crisp September morning. This is what happened, Baker.'

Finally, he's going to tell me, I thought.

'A man who looked near sixty, with a disfigurement of the arms, who had been jogging around the track, shouted in glee, his face open with joy at the sight of this joyful, beautiful, blonde woman stretching her hands to the sky and letting the water trace a tease along the bare parts of her. I too looked mesmerized at the sight, until the old man's voice drew me back to him. He had stopped jogging and jumped on the track, yelling, *It must be cold, it must be very cold. Is it cold?*

'And I looked again, first at her as she smiled at him and let him watch her rhythm, then back at him.

'Her neck stretched like a flower's stem, the light of the spray magnified, a baroque halo about her smile, and the man, the man jumping and turned fully toward her, forgetful of his maimed body, shouting *Is it cold, is it cold?* His face rang with delight, hers with simple pleasure, and I knew that for years to come, he would lie in bed and remember what he had seen with joy, joy through all his possessions, if he had any left, through the years to come, if he had any left.'

The coat stirred. The teacher looked at me for the first time since beginning the story. I saw the flames reflected in his right eye.

He said, 'That is what happened, Baker.'

A tower clock could have announced away the seconds while I waited for the explanation to tie his story together. He made no move to speak.

I said, 'That's it?'

He nodded.

'That's the world-shattering event that taught you about love?'

He nodded.

'Teacher, you leave me cold and feeling the depth of this hole. Where has your teaching gone? You've taught me absolutely nothing of importance except some things about you that I'd rather not know.'

'I don't teach any more. I live. Living is my business now. I don't have to explain anything to you, especially to someone like you.'

Ah, now he had angered me. Let his power make him clever, ridiculing me. Not the thing to do to the baker. I reached for the shovel. My blood faster.

'Now, now,' I said, 'be careful of what you say. People could misinterpret that remark. Maybe it's time to dismiss class.' I raised the shovel.

If I frightened him, he did not show it. Standing up, he squared his face to mine.

He pointed to his hair.

'She is blonde. Have you seen her?'

'No.'

'Baker, you said "No" too quickly.'

'Don't treat me like one of your students.'

'She looks you straight in the eyes, even when she cries.'

'I haven't seen anyone like that.'

He said, 'Her feet are soft and round, and her calves firm from dancing.'

'I don't watch people dancing and I don't see many bare feet. I am in bed early and people sleep when I wake. I live in the dark.'

'She would stop to help a bird fallen from a tree, a moth trapped by a window. Have you seen anyone do that lately? She raises ducks and hens in the small field at the back of our house, where the sun shines most of the day.'

I said, 'I have seen no ducks or hens, no birds or moths.'

His eyes narrowed, eyebrows frosted, his exposed forehead bruised blue and black.

'Baker, I have not seen her now for a week. I don't know where she is. Do you know? Have you done something to her?' His eyes sailed with wet. He cried.

'I don't know,' I said. 'Look, I don't know what she looks like. The town is full of crowds. Everyone, you know,' I gestured, 'moves in groups. Everyone is frightened, hungry. You know that better than anyone, Teacher.'

'I'm talking to you about one of those people, Baker, just one.' His finger shook.

I shook my head with both hands on the shovel.

'Look, look, okay,' he swallowed. 'I have more information for you.'

'No—'

'Please—' the words strangled at birth.

'A flirt at dinner evenings but shy alone. The first to remark on the weather to fill an awkward silence, but never to talk away a quiet moment, before a view or a painting. Cries for lost children, a tree snarled up with creepers, a plant that did not survive the summer. What else can I tell you about her?' He put his finger to his mouth and frowned.

'No—'

'We married in a white chapel. During the ceremony, her hand held mine. I never told her that I loved her enough – I'm not the type, you see, I don't, I can't be that easy with women, but she understood my silence, that was her way with me.'

'Please—'

'I have so much to tell you.'

'I can't help you, Teacher. I would if I could.' I stuck the shovel into the ground and dug. *There's always work you can polish a bit.*

He shouted, 'You see, I never stopped loving her. She filled every day of my manhood, every ounce of it.'

INFIDEL

I heard orders and shouts from the edge of the field. The truck's engine rumbled. And above me and the teacher, through the wide mouth of the hole, stars burned in pitch black. Yes, the snow had stopped. The storm had passed.

But the teacher wasn't finished. As if nothing else were going on, he kept talking:

'One evening I saw her on the terrace – we have a small balcony in our flat. I sat in the living room fingering a book and watched her go out to take the evening air. It was chilly, the sun had just gone down, and her skin had that evening glow. So much about her was filled with promise: her mouth almost a voice, her fingertips almost a touch, the perfume on her hair forming around my caress.

'Even now I can still feel her lips on mine, even in this desperate place, the rough brush of her fleshy scent that drifted close enough to become a kiss. The pain I felt when she wasn't with me. The pain her presence brought that couldn't be dulled by a thousand embraces, promises. I was never content.

'Baker, I'm not sure if perfect union is possible between two people. Some poison separates them always, some elemental force that individualizes every soul and keeps it a seed's distance from every other. Even love itself preserves this distinction.'

'I don't understand everything you've said,' I said. 'But I've read about Tantalus.'

'Yes, Baker, you remember!'

I felt his stare and I knew that I was vulnerable here in the hole with all those rocks lying around above. Swearing, he lay down on his belly, stretched out flat, and put his head over the edge of the hole.

'Infidel!' he hissed. 'You are as plain a liar as a traitor!'

The word threw me back, made my stomach weak and hammered my jaws together.

I said, 'I have not seen your wife!'

THE ATTACK

The trees around the field formed their own black wall now, faintly illuminated with snow. I was in a hole with walls inside a hole with walls. All the way up to eternity was a wall. All the universe was a funnel down to me. Like a telescope. But whose eye was on the other side?

His hand found a rock. 'You have seen her. Your hand is somewhere in this, Baker.'

'I have done nothing to her.'

'My wife was my friend, you see. In the morning she kissed me awake. Now, these past two nights, when the walls threaten to collapse on me with loneliness, I miss my friend. She was my friend. What have you done, for the love of God?' He pointed a weak finger. His voice rose.

'Your fingerprints line this deed. And you will pay. I miss my wife, my friend. When it's late and I can't sleep, I stare into the dark for a long time. I just miss my friend. And just two days so far. What will life without her be like?'

I waited for his attack. I crossed my arms against the cold and to defend myself.

But he seemed to calm down and turned upward, spoke at the stars. I was glad that he'd lost me, at least for now.

He said, 'I remember her at dawn.'

Silence.

'I remember her every minute.' He put his head in his hands and wept, 'Oh God, where are you?'

This confused me. I asked, 'Are you talking to your wife?'

I should have said nothing, and only nothing.

He stiffened. 'Who else would I ask?' he said.

'I don't know,' I said.

He turned back on his belly and placed his hand on a rock. 'You don't know? You don't know? What don't you know? I'll tell you again, you pathetic beast. You know nothing. Everything and damn nothing!'

He shouted something else, maybe *Infidel*, as he grabbed the rock with both hands and heaved it into the hole. It missed. Already, his hands were on another, a smaller one, which he threw. I pressed myself against the wall of the hole as it thudded into the side a few inches from my head. Then some smaller rocks from the Khan and Fievez piles, one struck me on my chin, the other my left ankle. I yelled in pain.

'I did not touch your wife. You have the wrong man.'

'You are the man. And always, always,' he threw another rock, 'it's one like you.'

'Maybe she's alive. Have you thought about that, Teacher? Have you?'

He stood with a rock in each hand, panting. 'When I think that she may be dead I want revenge, but I'm too maddened with grief to accomplish it. I will leave it to others.'

I stayed close to the wall, eyes on the rocks. I said, 'The Chinese say that before you set out on the road to vengeance, first dig two graves.'

He stood, opened his hands and looked at me for a long, long time with only the cold night filling the world atom by atom, freezing it from any hope, freedom, warmth. Blood trailed from his nose and mouth.

'They are already dug,' he said.

'Is this my hole, Teacher?' I asked, pointing at my feet. I laughed then. I laughed first softly and then with spittle coming out between my lips and down my chin, and I scratched my beard and bent my head back and laughed. Laughing from inside the hole, laughing as I pointed at him.

'History is about survival, Teacher, and the survivors are the people who end up writing it. You'll be the proof of that. I will win this argument.'

He said, 'You can fit any facts to fit what you want to believe. That is the tragedy of the past. Still,' he unbuttoned his coat, 'I was wrong to assault you.'

'You can't hurt me,' I said, and I knew somehow then that he could never try to hurt me again, whether in the depths of a hole or face to face. As I watched him pull his coat off, I noticed that nagging feeling I'd had since this morning. Something loose but tense about him. A lot of men like him in the world. They break slowly from the inside, each day losing another slice from the surface, another tiny thread snaps, maybe the ties to being a child finally broken, and the last one snaps and someone gets on a train and never comes back, goes on the road and keeps driving.

I wondered how I had reached thinking about a highway in such a short time.

The teacher held the coat up.

'I'll give you my coat if you forgive me.'

He didn't wait for an answer, swinging it in the frozen air.

I shouted in disbelief, 'What the hell can I do with it? Keep your damn coat.'

'Take it!'

He threw his herringbone coat. It spread in the wind and wafted over the hole, taking up the whole sky, darkening the hole. I hacked at it with my shovel as one would wrestle with an umbrella in a storm. I raged.

'You thick maggot!' I roared. 'Good God almighty!'

I caught the coat dead centre with the tip of the shovel and pole-vaulted it over the edge and away from the two of us. It settled like a black butterfly on the desperate white of the field. Even though the coat no longer obscured the sky, the hole pressed in on me. I had to get out.

Jesus, to think I'd end up in a hole.

THE HAND

Night buried the field as the snow had, flattening every rise and fall. The world was made of black and white. The crowd by the wall still huddled in groups, probably sticking with the friends they had in ordinary life. And the soldiers, in their heavy battle gear, held cigarettes in their weatherproof gloves and cracked the dark with the odd laugh. Above me, the teacher reached down.

'Take my hand,' he said.

I felt how strong the teacher's hand was. It grasped mine and he pulled me up. I kicked at the wall to get purchase. The field swung into view, on its side as I crawled out on my side, then upright as I stood. The teacher and I said nothing for a few moments as we stood together in the night.

I saw the truck lights flood the lines of people who no longer spoke and hardly moved. They stared.

I saw the soldiers lean on the wall of the field, chatting.

I saw the dark horizon of the black trees above the white field.

I saw the stars and I saw my breath between the stars.

'For God's sake,' I said. 'What time is it?'

He bent his head, checked his watch. 'I think it's five, almost five.'

The two soldiers in the emplacement took the plastic covering off the heavy machine-gun emplacement. They drank from a bottle.

He said, 'Cigarette? I have two left.'

I bent to the match. In the flash of his strike I saw how blue my fingers were where the gloves had worn through.

He had a lot to say to me. I let him talk.

'You know, Baker, I often walked to this field in all sorts of weather and moods. I came mostly as a child, especially in the first cold winds of autumn. The geese stayed here before flying south. I could hear their cackles from way off. Some geese stayed longer than others, and in my heart I hoped that some might stay the whole winter, though I also knew that no one had ever heard of that happening. I fed them each day until I saw them flying in circles above the trees. As they circled for the flight south, I had the feeling in my child's heart that I would always somehow be alone.'

'We're all alone, Teacher,' I said. 'We're alone now even though we're this close. This is it. This is history.'

Someone shouted. The lines moved forward, towards the hole. Soldiers took up their rifles and followed the lines. The teacher stared at his cigarette. Mine was half way done. I didn't feel like finishing it.

He said, 'Let me tell you that I've always felt briefly that there's a life I've just lived but I can't get back to it. As if the life I should be living is very near, like a small lane in the countryside, but I've taken a wrong turn and I have no map and no one understands my language or is lost too. Strange, Baker, that I should tell you something like that, something I've never—'

'What? What?'

'Something I never told my own wife.'

'That you are lost?'

'That the right life and I lost each other. I missed a boat somewhere and I can't get another. But I can hear the shouts of the happy coming across the fields or down a river. That's my torture. Yes, maybe this is it, Baker. Maybe it doesn't get any better.'

'It doesn't, Teacher.'

'Always a question. Your wife's faithfulness, your job, the exact year of your death, the faces of your future children. Always a mystery.'

I said, 'Some things you can know for sure.'

As if I'd said nothing, as if I wasn't there, he kept going, a ton of words out of him.

'Sometimes I think that God's just a lingering memory, you know, a good memory from being young and happy and with no care. What do you think?'

I knew he was looking at me. I stared ahead. We were too close for eye contact like that.

'I don't know what you're talking about,' I said, but it didn't make a dent in his speech. There was no way to stop him now.

'Then you grow and you realize you can't remember enough of those happy moments, and a creeping horror whispers to your unconscious that you've placed those memories somewhere else, Santa, the fairies, a sunset, a melody, your dead friends, the boyhood home you can never go back to, your mother's face. Her voice in the morning, waking you.'

'What?' I asked.

He took another drag. His white shirt shone out of the dark.

'You must be freezing,' I said, 'without the coat.'

'The coat is yours.'

'Thanks,' I said, 'but I don't need it.'

He shivered. The night air had dipped. It would be especially cold tonight.

'I've always dreamed of coats, all the important dreams, I mean,' he said.

'What were the coats doing in your dreams?'

'I always wanted a girl. We've planned it, my wife and I. From the youngest age I had a dream. The dream is that I am walking in a field of wheat with a girl, maybe eight or nine. The evening sun, we walk silently hand in hand. I wear a tweed coat and baggy trousers. Her hair is blonde and my hand contains the dimensions of the entire world for her. She is a quiet child, which is just as well, for I'm not much of a talker myself.'

'That could be disputed,' I said. The man could talk an army off its feet.

'As her father, I would be gently distant; to her fears, a steady friend; to her hopes, an open hand.'

I said, 'I didn't kill your wife. I swear it.'

His hand brushed my shoulder. 'I believe you. And thank you. You needn't have said anything. I admire that.'

He held out his hand.

THE KILL

I kept my hand by my side.

'I'm sure we shouldn't do that,' I said. Shaking his hand would have placed me in a very awkward position. So many witnesses. The reports.

Standing at my side, he wept then, this educated proud man, this all-knowing historian who held my brother's life in terror and humility for years. Wept like a baby from his belly. His shoulders shook and his face pressed into his hands. He sniffed and snorted like a little pig, turned around and wiped his face, why, I'll never know.

He sobbed his way through another speech even if I wasn't sure he was talking to anyone but himself, or people only he could see.

'Baker, I left the womb without God. He called after me but I was in no mood for staying in there, living off that slosh with all those tiny parasites biting me. I wanted to breathe air. The tiny seed of his voice got lost and I haven't been able to find him. I tried to think what God might have been or could be. A child, a girl, wandering in me, sometimes a cry. An instinct of what is right and good. A feeling I have at least somewhere that such a person does exist, but I can't wait for her now, either. Maybe God is a child and wants to be heard. Yes. I've seen her then, often, if that's what God is.

One day a hand will slip into mine and a voice will say, *I've found you.*'

The crowd stopped walking at an order, and formed one line, with the front person less than fifteen metres from the hole, to our left. The truck turned so that its lights caught up with them. Their skin shone and so did the teacher's white shirt and so did the stars.

Something sliced into the snow near my feet. I felt through the milky cold snow and found a plastic tube. I held it up and saw the dull glow of glass, flicked the switch and shone the light in the teacher's face. He looked behind him into the hole, then at me; then he glanced at the crowd.

The two soldiers behind the heavy machine gun slid the lever and fed the first clip into the chamber.

'I have a question,' I asked the teacher.

He shivered from cold or from fright. I said, 'Why did you come here, Teacher?'

'I wanted to be the first,' he said, staring ahead.

'There have been others before you,' I said.

'I wanted to be the first today.'

'Why?' I said.

He looked into the glare of the flashlight. I thought I saw his mouth move: 'They'll shoot you too.' But I decided it was only the night wind, a flurry of air through the trees, a trick of the light.

'I have lived long enough,' he said.

I walked away about ten steps and waved the flashlight. The soldiers cracked two seconds of bullets. The teacher's skull flipped back, his mouth a toothy grimace, and his knees sagged. More cracks. Those bullets propelled him backwards into the hole.

Four at a Time

I waited as the echoes scattered into the forest and died, waited for the gun to swing. One of the soldiers lit a match to his cigarette, like a slow explosion, orange across the dirty snow. It faded, and in the silence, I felt for holes.

They hadn't shot me. That's the beauty of not finishing till dark falls. I'd have a chance to make it to the woods if they tried to shoot me.

I waved the flashlight into the dark again and walked to the hole, where I found the teacher; he probably slid down the wall and landed on his neck, twisted, dead before he hit the ground. I moved the light across him, a piece of meat, cut, smoking where the bullets entered him, one in the jaw, one in his index finger, and a couple in his chest.

The ones that killed him.

I picked up his coat and threw it beside him, not on him, because I had some words for him yet.

'Teacher, your history didn't do you any good,' I said, loud enough that they'd hear me. 'You are full of shit!' And then I said, quieter now, at his corpse, 'You've learned nothing. You could have got away, lived in the forest. You should have known what would happen to you. You are stupid. You know all these facts, you said you understood why these things happen, and yet you couldn't put them into a plan for survival. Your wife is alone. Maybe dead too. That means you're stupid. I have learned enough to survive. And I am no teacher.'

Someone in the lines cried out. Someone else said *Ssshh*.

I whispered, 'What did you want, Teacher? Remember all your questions? What did you want? This will cure your sleep paralysis. Bet you can't move now, either.'

He looked pathetic to me, staring at nothing in the flash-light.

'You will not live again, Teacher. You're first in, as you wished. You won't get out of this grave.'

I turned to the soldiers and yelled, 'Bring them up four at a time.'

I heard people cry. Not a single one tried to run away, except a boy, whose father held him back by his shirt collar.

By five-fifteen we had mostly filled the hole with the six lines of people. Some fell straight, some fell crooked. Another half hour to arrange and pack them and do the lime in the dark and cold. I offered to fill in the rest of the hole, but the soldiers told me to go home. I saluted and left in a march I hadn't perfected yet, and the snow was too deep anyway for good marching.

We left no sentries at the grave. After all, who would attempt an escape? It's really simple. The dead can't attack you. You don't need anyone to watch the dead.

PART IV

6:00 p.m.

THE TEACHER'S WIFE

Someone said we should get out of the field. Another said it would be after six o'clock before we got back, that we had taken far too long about it. The two soldiers loaded the machine gun into the truck and we were ready to leave.

As a baker, I always grow tired around this time of evening, but I refused a ride in the truck and walked back to town along the trail. Didn't like sitting close to people.

As the soldiers drove away, one threw me a coat from the back of the truck.

'Took it out of the hole for you,' he said. 'Good coat!' he laughed and pulled down the canvas top.

Although it must have had blood on it and was torn, I put it on my shoulders.

The snow had stopped and what was on the ground was freezing. The little flakes crackled under my boots, and ahead, the yellow lights of the town hung low. Half way between the town and the field, I stopped at a bend in the trail where the view was cut off. The snow gleamed and the trees rose stiffly out of it. I gazed around. So silent. I could have been the only person in the world.

When I reached the town, I passed the secondary school basketball grounds where the women and children were kept. I walked carefully along the chain-link fence. After a couple of days' detention, you can see their manner change. No playing, no idle talk, as if conversation had no point here. Sitting on the ground mostly, sharing blankets.

A woman glared at me through dirty blonde hair. I stopped, put my hands against the fence, curled my fingers through the steel. I walked again, looked around. She followed me with a stare, I think at the coat, maybe out of desperation or cold, maybe just out of nothing at all. I'm told that these states can occur in detention.

I walked back, motioned her over, and again after she refused to acknowledge me.

'Hey, you, the blonde . . . come here.'

What moves women is beyond me, but of this I am sure, it is gain or sustenance, as their situation requires.

So I have read somewhere.

She walked upright to the fence where I waited, out of pride I think, to show that she still could move herself, despite her pallor and the filth and smell in the yard, and all that after only a couple of days. You'd think they'd take better care of themselves. Not like they'd been kept there long.

I offered her a cigarette through the wire. Her eyes did not move from mine as she made a tiny shake of the head. Again, eyes darted to the coat. I watched her as I struck a match to the cigarette between my lips. In that spark of light I could see what a man would like in her, what many men had probably lusted after in their youth when she moved under their windows or past them in the street, a round face with strong cheekbones, big blue eyes and a long neck. Good ingredients in a woman.

I whispered, 'Are you married?'

She grimaced and stepped back.

I laughed and shrugged. I knew I wasn't the most handsome man in the world, and most women I approach spurn me or ignore my advances, hope I will go away. They laugh behind my back, all the town women, even the plain ones who normally couldn't afford to be so proud or choosy. Now it was my turn to laugh at them. I opened my jaws and laughed my bad teeth through the barbed wire fence and shouted again:

'Are you married?'

Of course, she turned away at that; how predictable, but no one could deny her that small piece of satisfaction in her situation. In this camp with the others, no news of the men. It all had to be difficult if not impossible to bear.

The cigarette tinged red a couple of times and I flicked the ash on the fence and into the yard as I scanned the concrete. Some cleared away the snow with sticks. The other inmates lay on their backs or on their sides, beating at themselves to keep warm. Bunsen burners, wool blankets, pots to boil water in. All this I noted in silence, and only then did I finish my question,

'To the teacher?'

A rock might have struck her, such was the force that whirled her around and brought her back, her face a torn line between hope and hate. She grabbed the fence and shouted hoarsely, 'You know?'

'Ssshhh!' I put a finger to my lips. 'Come closer, I can't tell you this. I can't be seen talking to you.'

She inhaled sharply, smiled, trembled, wept. She leaned to the wire till our faces almost touched and the heat of her breath warmed my ear.

'You know?' she whispered.

I said to myself, *Survival. Nothing to lose. Guess, baker. Yes, baker. Guess.*

'So you are the teacher's wife?' I looked furtively around us.

Her face opened and hope spilled out like an opened can of peas.

'Yes, yes, have you seen him? Where is he? I've been sick with worry, if you can only help.' Her hands clasped and loosened. Erotic, definitely. Kamic, sutric.

Such was the openness in her face that I was forced to turn mine fully to hers, something I avoid doing with people. That eye-contact thing. People want to know things and the eyes give much away, much that is false in women, much that is peculiar in men. I saw the hope of finding her man fill her like water does a clear, clean glass.

'Yes, I've seen him,' I said.

She said, 'We heard shots a while ago – did you? We don't know what's happening. No one tells us anything.'

THE ASTRONOMER

If I were not a baker I'd have surely been an astronomer, for I am fascinated by light and its absence. I know that to the universe, earth, even the solar system itself, is less than a millionth of one grain of sand in an as yet undiscovered desert. I have often sat by my ovens at dawn and watched the night sky linger, felt the earth turn with my loaves under the heat of the sun, and waited for a comet or asteroid to make a pinprick into the earth and destroy us under spirals of dust. I have read that the rock that will annihilate the earth is already on its way, perhaps loosened millions of years ago from the asteroid belt, the Ort Cloud, that they say lies outside the solar system. That rock might be a kilometre or two wide, will give a few days' warning at most. Or none.

And when it happens, it will be a coincidence. Like me with this woman, the guess.

An asteroid. Imagine the pandemonium. Ashen-faced reporters. People burying their money, raping, accounts settled, shattered men sealing themselves into graves, praying for a life after death, the real nature of humanity working its way to the surface of the skin past a lifetime of hesitation, dieting, mathematics, shyness, boys and girls, pricks and breasts, night and day that mean the earth is turning, yes, this is the end and not one other thing else. Where are you,

God? No answer. You can't do this to us? No answer. To hell with you. No answer.

The poets will burn their poems. Romance will be minced, manners mayhem, politics pushing and shoving and stabbing and screaming. Ah, yes, it'll all break down in a day, just like when you see a traffic jam and people start to break the law, ride on the pavements, swear at each other to get ahead, yes, it'll be the glorious final show for all humanity. God says, 'This is what I made. They do this after all they've done and recorded doing. They do just this.' Elders quake, rot their knees, whisper to themselves, '*The space rock will miss us*, there have been others, it's a warning, one yes, that's fine, I'll take this one warning, I'll be good, please let me live, can I get myself out of this one or is the balance too big with interest and everything at this point?'

And the statues they pray to will answer out of spite, all at the same time, but out of sequence like a badly dubbed film: 'I showed you all of this, and you took nothing. Under this rock I will break your church. The weak will be weak, the last will be last, the eye of the needle is an eye of a needle, and the needle has poison in it, and it is stuck in your vein, and I am God, and you are dead.'

LETTERS

Dead. I looked down at what was touching my hand: the teacher's wife's hand. I shivered at her touch, recoiled, wiped my hand on my shirt.

'My husband. You know of him?' she asked.

I said, 'I think I saw him today.'

'My God, thank God, thank you, thank you.' I saw the years fall off her. Like a child, she smiled and cried at the same time.

I'd never learned how to do that. I didn't pull away, though I wanted to.

'My mother touched me once after I grew up,' I said to her. 'She wanted to stroke my hair and her fingers touched it but she didn't stroke it and then she pulled her hand away. She was my mother.'

The blonde shook her head, 'I'm sorry.'

'We did not talk when my father came home. I watched him eat, this big man with white hair, not sure how to make a word come out that he would respond to. I learned to speak in short gasps and to figure out what I wanted to say in advance, to avoid criticism, to increase the odds that he would accept what I said. He ate noisily, eyes to his plate and spoon, and the words I couldn't say piled up in my stomach, made me breathe all funny. I learned to talk to myself and watch the conversation as if I was another person. I moved away from my body just a little, just an inch. I remember the day it happened: everything felt strange for an instant, I felt dizzy, the trees blurred, a rush of strange blood in my head, and I was evicted from inside myself and replaced with a deader version of me. I tried no more. At home, we sat drinking and eating silently. I knew this was not the way other boys' parents behaved. Then my brother was born and I waited for him to grow up and then I played with him and I stopped talking to myself, but I never got back inside myself. I am easily frightened. That's what I mean to say.'

I think I said none of this to her. But I definitely said it to myself for the first time. I *think* I might have said it to her.

She sounded desperate. 'I'm sorry, did I startle you? I'm so sorry.'

'Yes, you did. A letter might be best,' I said.

'I have nothing to write with, and no paper.'

'Here.' I found a pen in the teacher's coat and tore a page from the small notebook in my pocket. 'Write on this. I'll make sure he gets it. I promise.'

She bit her lip and took a step back, stared at the page with tears on her eyes.

'We don't have time,' I said. 'We'll be noticed. Damn it, write quickly!'

She shook her head and laughed with relief, 'I can't, so fast.'

'Okay, write the most important thing. You have one minute. Listen—'

She turned her back.

'Listen. You have one minute.' I angled a glance to each side along the fence. I thought I had felt some papers in the inside pocket of the coat. I decided to wait until I got home before going through the pockets.

She lay on the ground and wrote four lines that I could count, creased the page and pressed it through the fence. She said, 'I cannot thank you enough. Perhaps after this is over, my husband and I can get to know you better. When things are back to normal.'

She stroked my fingers as I took the page from her – they might have been knives, such did my stomach clench itself.

She said, 'I know you, don't I?'

I pressed my hands to my jacket and bowed my head.

'Nothing is unforgivable,' she said.

I looked into her eyes. 'Nothing?'

'Nothing,' she smiled.

Her face was softer, some of the worry had drained out of her, her skin shone through the dirt. I whispered, 'What you've just said is a great relief to me.'

'I'm glad for you.'

'Well, it's not what you think. They shot your husband this evening. I was made to watch. I couldn't do anything of course.'

All this I whispered. I held her gaze, watched it worm back into worry and crawl into the grief that reached out its claws and tore at her face.

She tried to scratch at my hand, but the letter was safe on my side of the fence.

'That letter, give it back to me.'

Strange, I hadn't seen her mouth move. If I didn't know better, I'd say she had hate somewhere in that head of hers. Women can be like that, playing the game of masks with men. Never married myself, too much to learn to get that right and not enough time, anyway, when you have to drag yourself out of bed at four in the morning and be alone when everyone is going out for a drink or watching television. The tables turn and now suddenly it's not fair that I, the lonely baker who had to feed the town, now feeds off the town. They can't have it both ways. A little bit of power changes hands and suddenly it's all wrong, even though no one comes out and says it.

With the letter safe in my hand, I waved it at her. 'So, wife of the teacher, eh? You should have been in the other camp, the one that went to the field today. Never mind, tomorrow you'll get to visit it, the field.'

'Where——' She couldn't get words out. She looked finished.

She shook her head, slowly, so slowly she might have just shook it and not meant anything.

'What happened to you?' she asked.

Again, her mouth did not move, disconcerting, as if someone else was speaking from a distance.

Her hate was too big for her own body. That was my quick theory anyway.

I've read about this phenomenon of war: people walk around, wring their hands after an explosion; then they sit down twenty minutes later and die. Others will talk with you after they've had an accident or been badly hurt; then they'll tell you casually that they're about to die, and they do, just like that. Other people see too much and can't take the weight of their own emotions, so they go out of their minds to get some space, leave a vacancy behind them, a boarded-up tenement, a person who's seen better times. And some survive everything intact and don't go crazy until ten, fifteen years later, when they're holed up in a supermarket or training a gun barrel from a clock tower.

You see, I've read that the enemy never quite goes away. Like a drug you've taken or your first serious girlfriend. It pops out of a brain cell a decade later and says, *Remember me?*

I left her at the fence and arrived at my front door in five minutes, the beauty of a small town. I showered and dressed.

At six thirty I read her letter in my armchair.

Strange. No directions. No version of *Here I am, where are you?* She had sixty seconds and look what she wrote. Later, I read it again as I lay in bed waiting for sleep, my boots and socks drying before the log fire. The words I could understand, and their order, yet something seemed amiss. Her husband, the teacher, his name was missing. She only gave as author her initial. It was as if she were writing to herself. That she knew he was dead before I told her. Not to write to her love, but of love, a definition in her mind made of something they did together a long time ago. What was she doing? The covers tangled in my legs and I kicked myself free, rolled out of bed and put the kettle on the stove. What was her plan? After the water boiled I made hot strawberry tea and watched from my balcony the half-moon spread light on the town's steeples and empty houses, the snow that evened everything and made everything simple.

I thought of the teacher and his wife and their strange manner. Those two were a pair. He seemed to think that history, the subject to which he gave his life's work, was more than dates and personages and places, which I could accept up to a point because that argument was his final testament. He knew he was going to die; but what was all the talk for? We could have made a deal. Teachers have a lot of money, and people can fall into a grave alive as well as dead. We could have made a deal.

Last to be shot. Wait until we'd gone for the night, creep out of the hole and away with him into the night. I'd tell no one and pocket a nice piece of change.

And as for her, she wrote herself a letter. If it really was meant for him, why not give him information to help him find her?

My brother told me that the teacher once asked them to imagine living hundreds of years ago. Each person in the class chose a place and time. After the discussion, the teacher said that it was impossible to imagine correctly, since the signs and concepts of the time did not survive the passage of time itself. Of course we laughed at another of the teacher's idiot ideas, but now I imagined doing the teacher's experiment.

I rewound the night to the previous day, faster, faster, the nights and days lasting a second each and then ten to a second, the streets full and drained of people, lawns and trees blooming and dying ridiculously fast, like something breathing. The town stripped down to nothing and then just fields and then grass. The colours evaporated to new colours. The birds singing differently (although I had not heard birds in the town for days now). Children ran backwards to their birth, the dead themselves not yet born. Maybe the future rolls up from behind us like a wind, blows the past ahead into the horizon before us. Harvests turn to seed, marriages to first dates, music to ink, to ideas. And here was the funny thing, if the rewinding of time proceeded, I would see only what I already knew of the teacher and his wife: they'd leave their graves, he first, she running under the sprinklers on the morning of the running track, back further to the time they met. All I noticed is what I already knew. Why would I need to know more? It's nothing I can use.

He was a man who waited for history to come to him and say, *Here I am, the vision from your dreams, your decades of study, I have come to tell you that I am real.* Stuff like, 'Your heart is not in vain. You will not disappear. Love survives somehow and finds you. You will see your parents again. You will be with your wife. Have tea with Marco Polo. Ask Heidegger what he was talking about.'

Here was another problem. When the teacher took off his coat I saw how muscular he was under the shirt. The teacher, yes, strong, well proportioned; he could have beaten me, killed me in the hole, if he'd wanted to. For some reason, he didn't want to.

Thought too much, that's why. Too many choices is the same as paralysis.

Then I had a fright.

Wait, the coat.

What had I felt in the coat? I grabbed it from the hallstand and went through the pockets. Three envelopes, I knew I'd felt something.

I added hot water to the tea and sat by the fire, my toes close to the flames. I opened the first envelope. A letter, typed, beginning with 'Dear Student'.

Your essay on Schopenhauer's *World as Will and Idea* is remarkable for a young man. I remember being your age and can identify with many of your experiences, though when I was seventeen I was hardly as talented as you. For five years I have had the pleasure of

watching you improve as a thinker and writer, and
you must forgive me if I venture to observe that in
recent times you have seemed troubled and even
distant, not just in class but between the lines of the
very fine essays you have written for me this term.

It is a wonderful evening tonight. My wife is at the
opera. I stayed at home and have just heated a
wonderful apple pie and poured a fresh cup of tea. I
am easily pleased! I wanted to write to you and
perhaps to myself. Permit me this one act of
selfishness, to share with you a few things I have
learned. I am over twice your age and one does come
across some useful truths as one ages, although I am
never sure what the truth is. (I know that your
beloved Schopenhauer would have something to say
about that.)

Whatever your troubles, if indeed they have visited
you, they will pass. Yes, they will be replaced by new
ones, both great and small, yet all pass as does the
hangover that produces the immortal words 'Never
again'! Your calamities each reproduce the desire not
to experience any more pain. But life does find a
way to go on and pain is inevitable. When I was still
a very young boy a woman who was engaged to a
local boy died from a haemorrhage. Very sudden, no
time for goodbyes, preparations. She just died. Her
fiancé slept by her grave for two days, utterly
distraught, and refused any and all attempts by friends
and family to persuade him to go home. Finally they
came and dragged him away. He fought them all the
way to the car. Five months later he was married to a
local girl. Did he stop loving his fiancée? Of course

not. He just added new love to his life. Sorrow and joy: one does not contradict the other. The world is not black and white, and please do your best to resist all those who will have you believe it. Such a belief will cause you confusion and suffering. Be ready for change and you will change. For every breath you expel is replaced by a new one without any thought by you. In the same way, life takes care of you even as you sleep. You don't have to be watchful or anxious. A pen will write whether you squeeze it tight or hold it gently.

Perhaps you have fallen in love. Wonderful! Let its light shine on your mind and brighten your thoughts. Don't pretend to be something you're not. Don't act. Contradict yourself! Be honest, even if it makes you look weak. Be strong, even when it makes you look arrogant. Avoid mediocrity: it's the dark side of the crowd. Try not to speak in clichés, even if approved by those in authority. As far as feelings are concerned, I have come to think that people are the same everywhere. Everyone has the same problems. You are not alone. It is just that your friends may not have the words to put those experiences and feelings into place, so you all grow not realizing how similar you are. At every corner a new world of love opens. And without love, my dear student, history and everything in it is dry and dusty rubbish. Love may indeed be all sweet chemicals and nothing to do with divine intervention or a cherub with a bow and arrow. But let your heart enjoy it.

Such a long letter! Yes, I have written to myself as much as you. Perhaps I shall not now place this in the mail. I may keep my silence and wait until you graduate and go to university and meet you for coffee in the café that you and I both know so well. Then we can talk as men about life. And then I will bring you home to my wife's cooking, which she loves to do and for which I remain eternally blessed, as this is but one of her gifts to me, none of which I deserve. Not one. But that too is joy.

Although our province has experienced much pain in the last while, it will pass. This war will run itself out. The sun will shine again. And the will, as your philosopher friend might say, the will to experience life will blossom anew. Don't be afraid of life. Walk beside it, tell it your dreams, tell it your fears. Life can change anything. You will be happy. Use the telescope. Know what I mean? Point the telescope.

I read the teacher's letter twice through and shook my head. Is this a man talking? What a confused, illogical letter. 'Then we can talk as men about life'? Probably some infatuation with a student. A male student. *Of course*. All those intellectual types have that streak in them. That's what I've read, anyway. As far as I'm concerned, if you point your damn telescope you'll see a big dark patch called the void. Space.

The town was too quiet. I drew the curtains and put another log on the fire and tight balls of paper at the sides to help it burn. Seven o'clock. I should have been hungry. Usually I would go to bed at this time. Why wasn't I hungry?

I thought that perhaps the teacher had reached the point of his own insanity, the pressure of all that thinking. I could

have told him. I should have told him before he died that my
brother liked him but thought him much too intense for his
own good. Yes, my brother liked him.

The second letter was addressed to 'My Dear Niece':

On my eleventh birthday I received Orca as a gift, a
cat with a ribbon on her collar who lived on the farm
and spent a good bit of each day in front of the
woodstove. Her owner had died and she needed a
new home. My parents said it would be good for me
to learn to care for something. Orca never made a
sound, didn't play that much. That was her way. She
sat on my lap and that was all she wanted. We
accepted each other. A couple of months later I came
home to find that she had been poisoned with rat bait
in a neighbour's yard and that my sister had already
buried her. I was sad beyond belief, a wreck for days.

I grew up with cats; there was always one in the
family home. When they went missing, we'd search
for days, drop everything and search until we found
them. They lived with us for many years and when
they died, it was exactly the same as losing a life-long
friend: devastating. What we grieve most about lost
pets is their solitude, their silence. They can't talk to
us, and they bring that silence with them when they
go. I know you are sad. But your own little cat is on
his journey. Let yourself be sad for him and don't try
to hide it.

That was his letter to his niece. A cat. What did this man
have in his head? I opened the last envelope. The third letter
wasn't addressed to anyone:

Two days now, and I don't know where you are. I think they will come for me today. But I have looked through the telescope from far ahead in time, and I see you still, now and for ever, in my heart. That's all I see, all I want to see. I cannot bear the thought that death is the end of us. The telescope will help me find you. I have placed myself in the future, where I will wait. And I will find you.

All very touching. No information anywhere. Nothing I could use. I tossed the envelopes into the fire and felt the increased heat on my toes.

I shut the balcony door against the bitter night cold air and jumped into bed again, grateful for the trace of warmth left on the mattress, grateful that I still had my home to sleep in. The occupiers understood the day-to-day functioning of war. They knew how things worked. There was the useful side of things, and the useless side. I was on the useful side. God, to be lying in a blanket on the concrete of the basketball court out in those temperatures.

And this, this too bothered me; I had talked to the teacher's wife about my parents. I had never talked with anyone about my parents before.

I would have to be more careful.

I took her letter and read it again:

My sweet love, run with me again through the sprinklers, remember that? The day I knew we could be together for ever. Try to think of me as I will, with all my heart, of you. I will wait. From a distance, across time itself. I've never loved you more, my dearest love. S.

Her name? I checked the note. I remembered her now. She came into the shop with the teacher once. Ran in after him, actually. A day in early October, last year, a bright breezy day after the market. Said she'd got him a present. Held it up to him, her face shining. A china cup with flowers. The cup was quite nice. Bought it at the market from a traveller, she said. She held the cup up to him, and then I noticed something that made me stop, my loaf half covered in the brown wrapping paper. She held the cup up to the teacher. He smiled and went to take it, but she backed off a step and shook her head. She motioned to her lips, giggled, and held the cup to his.

It was steaming.

'I've made tea in it,' she said.

Truly, that made me stop what I was doing and stare. I'd never seen or read anything like it.

She turned to me and said, 'It's my husband's birthday today. He's shy for his age.'

And what did I, the baker, do? I bent to the wrapping because she smiled at me and held my gaze too long for my comfort. She had bones that made her face look like china. I thought then, and this horrified me, that I could drink life itself from her face. The thought came from nowhere and that scared me more.

Her name? Her name was on the note she wrote. One letter.

I folded the letter, wondered if I should throw it away, burn it. I decided to keep the letter on the table by my bed.

I burned his three letters.

Tomorrow or the day after they'll escort the women from the camp to the field, fill in the final hole and then they'll let me go, release me from service, as promised. Get back to baking, minding my business, walking close to the town walls as I go to work. Now to sleep. They'll remember that I was a baker by trade, and that's something useful in hard times, when there's a lot of marching and hauling machinery to be done. They'll need someone who can make bread, and I'll remind them of that when the last body drops and my shovel falls useless on the snow.

ACKNOWLEDGEMENTS

I wish to express my thanks and deep appreciation to those who provided support, shelter, and advice: Wendy Sherman, David Marcus, Giles Gordon, Christina Nalty, Andrea Lauren, DeAnna Rivera, Michelle Collotta, Michael Carragher, Scott Lax, Alice and Noel, Natalie Remington, Richard Donovan, Alison, Isabella, and Johnny Michael.

The baker disappeared shortly after the events described in this novel. Curious neighbours found library books and research notebooks in his bedroom. He had borrowed *Storm across Asia* by Henry Wiencek as well as Robert Marshall's *Storm from the East*, both documenting the Mongol conquests. He probably checked *The World's Worst Atrocities* by Nigel Cawthorne for details of King Leopold's reign in the Congo. As for the Wounded Knee episode, it appears that he consulted, among other sources, Rex Alan Smith's *Moon of Popping Trees*. He possessed a number of translations of *The Art of War*, and apparently mixed in some of his own, and he most likely found his references to Count Fulk and medieval European life in William Manchester's *A World Lit Only by Fire*. The baker must have located information about inventions in *The Timetables of Technology*, edited by Bryan Bunch and Alexander Hellemans. *The Faber Book of Madness*, edited by Roy Porter, was most likely his source for David Hume's letter.

I heard my first vivid details about the Dresden bombing from Dipfel, a German herbalist who harvested mushrooms in the Bavarian woods in the late seventies. R. H. S. Crossman's essay 'Apocalypse at Dresden' is an excellent account and appeared in *Esquire Magazine* in November 1963.